*Thomas –
Thank you for your support. May your inner light always* <u>GLOW</u>*!*

Peter

Glowing Up Gay

Peter Leahy

Glowing Up Gay

Thanks –
Thank you for your support. May you never light always Glow!
Peter

Copyright ©, Peter Leahy 2023

All rights reserved. No part of this book may be reproduced in any form by any mean, electronic or manual, including information storage and retrieval systems, without permission from the author

PROLOGUE

In many ways I feel naked now. By the end of this book, you will know all of my challenges, insecurities, disappointments and how my life was screwed up before I turned it around and finally got things right. You'll learn about my bankruptcy, my stomach problems, my academic struggles and other heartbreaks. Why am I revealing this – am I a glutton for punishment?

I am disclosing these to provide a complete story of my Coming Out journey. All of these events are true and I'm providing my perspective on experiences that shaped my life and the self-assured and happy man that I am today. Admittedly my memory isn't perfect but I'm confident that I've accurately shared what occurred at the time and my feelings about it. This story is not sugar-coated; this is what happened to me, this is how I remember it.

When I think about the decades that I punished myself and hid my true identity, the word 'ALONE' is tattooed on my brain. That was the emotion that enveloped me. I had no one that I felt I could trust with my secret, no outlet to validate my feelings. Reflecting on WHY I'm writing this and WHO I want to target and WHAT I want them to feel, the most important gift that I hope I can impart is a sense of belonging, that whatever struggle(s) you have, there's no reason to do it by yourself. Reaching out and being vulnerable to people is scary and you may fail at it the first time. But you have the power to try again, to find your path to happiness. To find the courage you need to become the best version of yourself, even if that means leaving everything and starting over.

> Courage
>
> is the ability to
> choose the p
>   a
>   t
>   h
>   that leads
>   into the unknown.
>
> @simonsinek

PS – I must be confident, because I share loads of personal stuff that still embarrasses me to this day, but I felt it was important to paint a complete picture of me; past, present and future.

ACKNOWLEDGEMENTS

For a man that came out of the closet in his 40's and publicly declared his attraction to men, I'm going to surprise you. I must begin by thanking a whole bunch of women in my life who helped me get to where I am today. It starts with my mother, a woman who continuously advocated on my behalf. While reflecting on my life I now see her in a different light (admittedly more critical), but that does not minimize her impact on my personality and one of her gifts to me, my genuine thirst for knowledge. My sisters played critical roles in my journey, my escape from my former life. As you'll find out in my story, I was lost and needed my family to support me on my path to happiness. Thank goodness they were there to set me "straight." Yes that's a curious figure of speech and yes I love Dad Jokes. My work wife gets a whole chapter devoted to her - don't be jealous ladies! I was a frightened puppy when I first came out and needed a friend, mentor, confidante and voice of reason. She was (and is) the total package - I am forever grateful for her guidance. This book was called "Lena Story" during its development, named for another friend. This idea started with her – she challenged me to organize my thoughts and just start writing. I did just that and realized that I loved what I was doing – I had something to say that I hope you will enjoy.

It's time for the boys – Terry provided tremendous guidance in helping me with tone, narrative, editing and publishing logistics. Like many of my angels, you came into my life at the perfect moment and I hope you know how much I appreciate you and your phenomenal guidance. Most of my friends are gay men in the Atlanta area that I didn't know ten years ago. I was fortunate to find a community that embraced me and helped me graduate from Baby Gay status. My definition of a friend is someone who makes you a better version of yourself and I am lucky that some good ones dropped into my lap. And for my husband, thank you for loving me and for letting me love you. I wish we had met earlier in life so that we could have even more memories together. I am thankful that our paths finally crossed and I look forward to a lifetime of love, laughter, morning coffee on the veranda, antiquing and fighting over the thermostat.

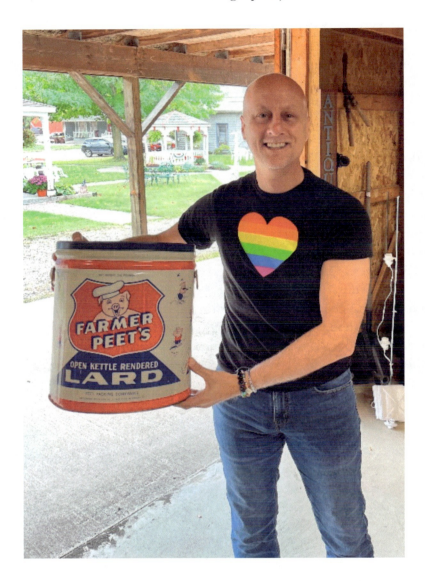

FOREWORD

As any helping professional will tell you, there is something so extraordinary about watching your student, patient or client experience growth that prompts a complete life change in who they will be. The new growth can change their path, their goals, the traits they emulate in others and the people they look to for love and the way this person sees life.

I received a similar gift of observing your author experience his renaissance when he came out as a gay man. It's not easy to relay his complete change ---I think of Dorothy from the classic movie Wizard of Oz, after the tornado lands her house, she stands in her black and white existence as she opens the door to the colors and whimsy of Oz .

Coming out is not easy. The decisions involved in becoming your true self are complicated. You mull over questions like : when do I share my true self? How do I explain to my spouse and children that the heteronormative life we have known is over? What can you say to the people you love that will explain your need to live authentically, when it will change much of what you all know being together?

I could closely relate to Peter's coming out experience because I too was moving in a similar path. When Peter and I met as online friends, the similarities we shared as husbands and fathers and breadwinners were bonding. We could easily relate to how hard we tried to be the person we felt society wanted us to be. The older version of Peter was bright, kind and committed to his family and his work. Anyone could see Peter was a man on a mission --striving to provide for his family. But he was also man on a treadmill—moving –but stuck. Talented in his field—yet frustrated, controlled and unexpressed as a person. His true self was dormant. He wanted to love who he was but he could not yet embrace the secrets that made him unique. When I read his story, I was sad to see how much he hated himself, I wished I could have helped him more.

Once Peter began his evolution, I was a stunned observer. His transition was in fast steps, but it was miraculous! He was colorful, he was open to new ideas . He was emotive and expressive of a brand new being who was loving himself—even with the challenges of coming out. You couldn't help to love this man who was revealing his peacock feathers! And he was his authentic self, happy and funny!. I am proud of Peter in a way few people can understand—once he worked to reinvent himself and he began reaching out and sharing his colors with the world....making his city and his profession more accepting for others living with the LGBTQ+ experience. Peter's story is his journey to the authentic self-love we all want.

Most of us have experienced challenges to being accepted in our families, our schools, our houses of worship. The isolation we feel from verbal bullying and emotional abuse contaminate our sense of self . It can drive us into unproductive relationships and harmful behaviors. But we can move from the world of shadows and hurtful ideas that fill our heads to a healthy sense of self and hope to joining the world and being alive in it!. I hope you are able to see Peter's story as one of hope that allows you to be your unique self, able to overcome life's challenges. Authentic happiness is out there!

Larry Schwarz – Miami, Florida

Gay Dad / Educator / Mental Health Professional

TABLE OF CONTENTS

Chapter One – June 2013 - 44 Years in the Closet, then Busting Out!

Chapter One-and-a-Half – So…When Did You Know?

Chapter Two – October 1987 – It Was A Tragic Love Story

Chapter Three– October 2000 - A Heartbreak, The Miracle, My Greatest Accomplishment

Chapter Four - 1970's-1980's – Triple-Trouble, Family Die-Namics

Chapter Five – A timeless story - Family Lost, Family Found

Chapter Six – March to June, 2014 – Let's Combine a Divorce AND a Bankruptcy AND another lawsuit

Chapter Seven - December 2019 – Control, Control, and Even More Control

Chapter Eight – January 2018 – The Curious Adventures of Trivia Man & Quiz Bowl Boy

Chapter Nine – June 2015 – Clothes Maketh the Man – Mr. Speedo Man

Chapter Ten – February 2017 - Boston Sports Fans – from Lovable Losers to Obnoxious Sore Winners

Chapter Eleven – October 2004 – How the 2004 Red Sox Rehabilitated New England and the Leahy's

Chapter Twelve -October 2015 – Mildred Sweet Mildred

Chapter Thirteen– December 2014 - Dating in the 21st Century + Gay Apps – What the Heck is Going On?

Chapter Fourteen – July 2013 - Going to Provincetown, Finding Gay Bear Mecca

Chapter Fifteen – 26,690+ Snapshots of a Life Well Lived and my 'Cerebral Music'

Chapter Sixteen – September 2013 - Unlocking a New Passion, Creatively Cooking for Health

Chapter Seventeen – July 2015 - Marriage Equality and My Fur Baby

Chapter Eighteen – My Late-Blooming Education and Corporate Follies

Chapter Nineteen – How My Marketing Career Blossomed in the Right Environment

Chapter Twenty – If At First You Don't Succeed…

Chapter Twenty-One – August 2020 - Building a Life with the Bear of My Dreams

Chapter Twenty-Two – My Continuing Metamorphosis; Waiting for My Children to Come Home

Chapter Twenty-Three – Admitting When You Need Help and Asking For It

Appendix

    Unsent letters to my ex-wife and my father

Chapter One

June 2013 - 44 years in the Closet, then Busting Out!

Here's the thing that most straight people don't know – there are rules about being gay, a whole different language from the straight world. You often classify yourself and others based on physical characteristics (twink, daddy, chub) and there are animal names for different body types (bear, wolf, cub, otter, puppy). There are even catch phrases (Mary) that guys will use – it might be a compliment to a friend or throwing shade at some tragic guy across the room. It's not right or wrong, just different. I kinda wish that there was a manual or handbook or rainbow pamphlet when I came out. Why hasn't someone created the "Rainbow Road Interactive Workbook" or the "Destination Dorothy Guide for Baby Gays?"

But I'm getting ahead of myself. Let's start with the basic premise – I was in the closet for over four decades and admittedly, I can't give you an exact reason. I wasn't raised in a particularly religious household. There was no specific family pressure to get married or have kids. I was just afraid of being different. I knew that in my ecosystem, being gay was bad. Not "Going to Hell" bad, more like "You Are Not One of Us" bad. In my upbringing, part of the 'othering' of gay people was that they also didn't exist, they weren't in our community. We rarely saw them on television and if they were featured, they were ridiculed. They weren't serious people, they were two-dimensional. They were a joke.

The cherry on the top of this homo sundae was shame – I knew the type of men that interested me sexually, and I was one billion percent embarrassed by it. I didn't want it to be true. I knew that what I felt was wrong, that I was defective in some way. I am attracted to (and am now thankfully married to) a BEAR. In gay parlance, a bear is a heavy-set guy who is often hairy. The gay classification knows no bounds, as there are probably a dozen bear variations / varieties out there (Ginger Bear, Daddy Bear, Muscle Bear, Bear Cub, etc.). I didn't know any of this until I saw pictures and read about it on the Internet. Seeing that there was a name for the kind of man that attracted me was a relief – I wasn't alone, I wasn't weird or a deviant.

Until my awakening I was determined to live in the straight world – to make it work. I wanted to live an ordinary life just like everyone else – fall in love, get married and have kids. Just be normal. So, I created a persona that attempted to fit in. I liked being around girls and eventually fell in love with my wife. There was a part of me that was too scary to acknowledge, so through a lot of mental effort, I willed that part of me away. I didn't want it to be true, so I tried to pretend that it wasn't. For over forty years, I orchestrated a process of denial, masquerade, assimilation and settling. I tried to fit in and have straight friends and I sort of did, but it was a losing proposition. The number of arguments that I had with myself was staggering. I reasoned away most of my decisions about living this lie that I was doing my best, that I wasn't hurting anyone.

But I was alone. I mentioned the illusion of straight friends but the embarrassing truth at that time was that I had no real friends. My wife and I would often make friends, usually a couple with small children, but invariably they would drift away, it wouldn't last. Looking back, I wonder if we presented some type of weird vibe. Was there a sense about us that produced a strange feeling, like we were damaged goods? This lack of social interactions was bad for my health. I'm a classic extrovert, but after a while my social circle was the kids and my wife – no friends, no life.

The process of living a lie took its toll on me in a weird, sad way. While I was pretending to be someone that I wasn't, I was also living a lie financially. We created a false lifestyle through credit card debt and essentially "buying" our happiness and living beyond our means to present a normal face, at least to the outside world.

How did I manage my finances? The first thing was living month-to-month. It wasn't living, it was surviving. The first four days of each month were the best. The direct deposit hits, you can breathe easy that night, you pay the bills and have money to spend. That's what my other half did, using a combination of debit and credit cards. She bought what she believed was necessary for our house and our children and she was not to be questioned. The next (saddest) step was holding my breath until the 20th of each month. I didn't look at the bank account, I couldn't bear to see how small the amount was, see the money going down.

Unfortunately, I had built up such strong defense mechanisms that if I didn't see it, it didn't exist. So, when the 20th came around, it was time to develop the survival action plan: what's our strategy to make it to the end of the month? The plan had three components: (1) THE BASICS – food and gas – nothing else was allowed, (2) RETURNS – can we go back to the store and get credit, will they notice, (3) FINANCIAL GYMNASTICS – buying groceries on the last day of the month with a check or buying diapers with your medical spending card at Publix, then returning them to a different Publix for store credit.

Essentially, I had devolved into a zombie – I existed to make money for my family, to help parent our children and to clean the house on the weekend. Anything beyond that was considered a luxury. What hurts the most now is how I let myself be controlled, to give someone the power to decide WHERE our money was spent, HOW I was going to live my life, and WHEN I was allowed to leave the house. It was a dictatorship and I willingly went along with it. I was afraid to challenge the status quo – I felt relatively safe in my "straight world" bubble and the marriage stress and financial hardship were the price I had to pay to remain in the closet.

I felt like the world was against me, that our constant money troubles were typical and what other people had to deal with. Secretly I thought that our horrible financial situation was my fault. Not from spending beyond our means, but that our troubles were punishment for hiding my shameful secret. Denying myself was another form of internal punishment. Not spending money on myself was a way to remind myself that I didn't deserve to receive anything, and it helped us control our expenses too. I hated what I saw in the mirror every day, so why invest in it? Who's gonna notice? I didn't go to the dentist for nearly seven years. There's no money issue here – regular cleanings are covered by insurance – but I believed that I was a worthless piece of shit. When I finally went in 2013, they told me that the back of my teeth looked like coffee with cream. Another friendly reminder is that self-care is an important part of self-love.

There was an 'interesting' way that I manifested my unhappiness with myself, my shame of living a lie, and my embarrassment of being a financial failure. It's not pretty, but it shows what stress and anxiety and self-hate can do to you. I couldn't poop. Like for days at a time. When the issue first started, it was a pattern of hold vs. release. I couldn't go to the bathroom for 3-4 days, then that final day was such a relief. Multiple bowel movements later, I felt lighter and wasn't bloated. I felt like a real person. I was normal for about 24 hours. And yes, I went to multiple gastrointestinal doctors, had colonoscopies, and there was nothing there. Of course there wasn't – it was crippling stress – my goodness how did I not see it?

I employed a dietary coping mechanism – for the better part of 4-5 years, I had a liquid diet, except for the occasional restaurant experience. Solid food was the enemy – why eat things that may result in a bowel movement if you can't produce one? It got to the point that I had to make tough choices about what I put in my body – do I want to eat that roll before dinner arrives? Am I wasting those empty calories? If I sample the appetizer but then my main course makes me feel stuffed too quickly, have I made a wrong decision?

It sounds like an eating disorder but it's more like a coping disorder. Every part of my body was miserable and somehow the control that I was trying to maintain by hiding my secret became a weapon against me. Now my life consists of a typical pattern of eating, sleeping, drinking water, exercising, etc. All of these have a role and because I am internally happy, there are no crazy side effects. I like to say that now I 'live through love,' it's my lead emotion. Back then, fear occupied the number one position – like I was juggling multiple lies and persons. There was no time to just be happy or relax, there was always another crisis to navigate – remember, a financial hurdle was always 30 days or less away!

All this food and poop-related shit may sound trivial, but it defined who I was. I was a failure – even my own body didn't work anymore. And trust me, if you live month-to-month paying minimums on your credit cards and then you go out to dinner that you can't afford and you can't even enjoy your meal, your life pretty much sucks. Why spend money that you don't have on something that's going to deliver a negative experience?

Again, this was my life. It wasn't created overnight; it just became our slow-moving reality. And the weird thing was that I didn't question it, couldn't see that it was wrong, that it was unsustainable. It just became accepted that this was the way that we were going to ~~live~~ survive and that we just muddled our way through it.

Muddled is probably the most apt word that demonstrated who I was to the world. It's the Debbie Downer, the Eeyore that I was showing the outside world. I didn't like who I was, was embarrassed by the way that I was living, and was ashamed of what I felt inside, so my exterior shell reflected lukewarm coffee, slightly stale bread, or maybe flat diet cola. Was I depressed? Probably. I always felt like I technically wasn't unhappy - I had a job, a home, a spouse, and a boy and a girl – these together are the American Dream. This is what I wanted, but of course I hid a big part of myself to achieve it. I just wasn't happy. Knowing what I know now and how I feel now, I wasn't even in the same universe with happiness.

I'm hard on that old version of Peter – I think he's pathetic, a loser, a wimp. I know that it's me and in many ways I'm still the same person, but I also reject that Peter. I am slowly forgetting him. Again, is it healthy to think this way? Yes and no – part of the celebration of life and inner peace-joy that I embrace now is because of the demons that I have exorcised; that downright hopelessness that I felt for years, the sincere belief that my life was already over. Eventually, I came to accept that I wasn't ever going to be happy, that being myself was too dangerous, that revealing my true self to the outside world would ruin me, would take away everything that I knew, everything that defined me.

It is tough to admit this as an adult male, but I was in an abusive relationship. I let someone else control me, dictate our life, and have the final say in all decisions. I should add some context on how much I gave her all of the power in our relationship:

a) I traveled for work every 3-4 weeks and my wife was wonderful at taking care of the children, making all the meals and getting them and herself ready for school. Nearly the entire house would be clean when I got home. There was one blind spot – the kitchen. Normally I would come home and every single counter space would be covered in trash – some combination of dishes, leftovers, boxes – a real jumble of junk. The dishwasher would normally be empty, so cleaning that area and taking out the trash was my #1 job when I got home. If my time away was particularly stressful for my wife, I would come home to a clean house and spotless kitchen. What's the difference? My wife would throw away everything in the kitchen that was normally piled high on the counter into industrial trash bags and it was my job to 'rescue' and later clean the plates, silverware and glasses among the combination of garbage and food packaging. It was embarrassing and dehumanizing to sift through garbage in your own home.

b) Because I traveled for work, that was considered my 'me time' and I wasn't automatically allowed to have free time on the weekend. Said differently, I had to earn it. The house needed weekly cleaning (vacuuming, bathrooms) and the outside lawn maintenance was my responsibility, plus watching the children while my wife went shopping for the family. Remember, she's out there buying things that we probably don't need and spending money that we don't have and I'm stressing out on the financial gymnastics that I'll need to figure out later in the month.

c) This unspoken rule of the limits on Peter going out is best explained from this 2008 example. I had plans to go out TWO nights in a row – the horror! In both cases, it was with my only friend at work, also a dad with young children. One night we attended an Atlanta Braves game and the next night we had plans to see Spamalot (Monty Python musical). I didn't clear these back-to-back events with the wife and when she found out about the second night, she was livid and forbade me from attending. I had purchased the tickets and had to sheepishly drive to his house and provide a lame excuse of why I couldn't go. I can only imagine how he felt when I arrived – I was pathetic, I was not a real man, and we had a seriously fucked up relationship. This isn't a one-off example – it was the norm that her time away from the children was a necessity and any potential time away for me was a luxury.

It hurts just typing this – what made me so subservient, so submissive? Of course, I know the answer – fear. OMG did I fear everything and everyone. It's amazing that by having that anxiety, by not dealing with my problems, I wasn't living. I existed in a world that allowed me to appear as I belonged within it, but I was not a part of it.

Being outed was easily my number one fear. It wasn't safe for me to come out of the closet. Practically, it would not be good to be gay in a professional setting and internally I wasn't ready. You see all the stories today about teenagers or young children that are comfortable in expressing their sexual identity. Times were different then, but I must acknowledge that it was me that created this intense pressure. I wasn't ready to face a world, alone, and tell people that I was gay. I just wasn't ready to come out until I was ready. And when I was finally ready, I jumped in with both feet!

The irony is that I was already alone and coming out allowed me to find a place where I belonged. It may be obvious that we now live in a world that's more accepting than 8-10 years ago, but at the time I couldn't imagine that that world would ever exist. I couldn't see that the life I was living was a cage, a trap. But breaking out of that, breaking free of my fears was the right path for me.

Not dealing with my sad reality is exactly the opposite of what I do now – I live authentically and by truly loving myself and being comfortable with who I am, my world reflects that. I'm such a cliché – once I was finally free from what held me back, my world and the people that I encountered and accepted into my life, they were mostly good to me, good for me. I finally accepted the real me and the universe presented me with people who have become real friends, part of my extended family.

Another component of that non-existent gay handbook is how easy, affirming, and awesome it is to love your friends and to tell them that regularly. Of course, it's not romantic love, but coming out allowed me to tell them how much I loved them, and how much I valued their impact on me. Nearly every member of my social network helped build a part of me – it was both creating the new me and helping dissolve the old me. I can't believe I had been missing out on how to make friends, to be better connected with others. At the end of the day, it was about me loving myself. All the gays know RuPaul's famous line, "if you can't love yourself, how in the hell you gonna love someone else? Can I get an Amen!"

I'm no self-help guru, I don't have all the answers and didn't come into this enlightened state at an early age so that I can teach you my super-duper way of living your best life. No, I'm just a person who changed, who evolved in his 40's. It wasn't too late for me (thank goodness!) to finally be happy, to finally grow as a person because of positive people and experiences, as well as removing negative people and environments.

This change, this evolution - it started on one day – February 28, 2013. There's nothing special about that date, no specific event or memory that triggered it, but essentially it was my 'no looking back' day. I decided that I wasn't going to be unhappy anymore. That was the day that I told myself to not fight it - I was gay. I could say the word out loud to myself, that the life that I was currently living was a lie, ruining my health, and I needed to make dramatic changes to leave my imprisonment. It was like a prison break – I was escaping from everything I knew. I left my home a few months later not knowing what the future held. I still don't see it as courageous or anything like that – I was at rock bottom and I had nothing left to lose.

It took me months to come up with the courage to leave – man I was scared. I knew that I wanted to leave my wife, that I needed to remove myself from our toxic home, but I cried myself to sleep most nights because I didn't know how to break free. I was broken and convinced that I was a failure as a person. I wasn't straight but I certainly wasn't ready to admit that I was gay. Then came the day – June 13, 2013. Again, nothing special about that day. My mother-in-law was in town and we had planned a family vacation to Tybee Island.

Quick story about the family vacation – we rented a home near the beach and there were two buildings on the property – the main house and a one-bedroom apartment. Before you ask about the sleeping arrangement, it's weird. My wife and her mother would share a bed in the main house, where the kids would also share a bed. They wanted me to sleep in the apartment with the dog – what a metaphor. Again, this was just accepted as normal!

Back to the morning of the 13th – I'm in Nashville for work and I receive a call from my wife early in the morning, asking me why I haven't left yet. I told her I was on the toilet and hung up on her. She called back, furious that I would challenge her, and demanded that I come home immediately. I said something like "I'll get there when I get there" and we didn't speak again until I came home. There's no bravery here, I wasn't assertive. While driving from Nashville to our home near Atlanta, I put the cell phone in the trunk. I was afraid of her calling or texting me – I was afraid of the phone all the time because it had become a way to keep track of me, to make sure that I was always on call and could respond immediately.

Eventually I came home, to face the person who I had allowed to control me. After picking up a couple of items, all I said was 'I'm done,' jogging slightly to my car. Remember, I'm still deathly afraid of my spouse and didn't have the balls at the time to stand up to her, to challenge her. The funny thing is that I had a plan and didn't have one at the same time. I walked out the door with some work clothes and a coupon for a local Mexican restaurant. She followed me out the door, chased me to my car and pounded on the passenger side window of my locked car, asking me 'what was I doing, where was I going.' I then turned the engine on and out came this snide warning from her which is forever seared into my memory…'I'm going to tell your boss!' (yes, that was a threat to out me) Dripping with superiority, words like that had made me powerless in the past and kept me in check. But this time I just smiled and said 'OK' and drove away. PS – I also heard 'I'm going to report this car as being stolen' as I backed out of the driveway.

As I got on the highway, unsure of my destination, I didn't see it as the beginning of a new life, as a fresh start. I was petrified. I had no idea what the future held – I just walked away from everything I knew. I didn't have any circle of friends or support system. I drove to my work to take a shower (admittedly I had nowhere else to go) and I ran into my HR guy and he was staring at me – he looks surprised and worried at the same time. He's probably shocked because I had shaved my head the night before (one of the best decisions in my life – breaking free from male pattern baldness – removing my insecurity about my lack of hair). He says three things in rapid succession: "Peter, you shaved your head.

Peter, you look like you've lost weight. Peter, are you okay?" I blurted out that I was gay and had just left my wife. I said the word 'gay' for the very first time to another person outside of my siblings, and I had only told them a couple of weeks earlier. This was not an 'out and proud' moment. I didn't feel confident, didn't feel like I was a real gay, whatever that was. At that moment I felt like I was a fraud and a failure. What I realize now is that I was finally taking responsibility for who I was and my situation, but at that moment I guess I was trying out this 'truth' idea. Can I say the word gay? Can I trust people with my secret that's not a secret anymore?

Now for the shocker – he said, "it's okay Peter, I'm gay too." I was floored. He was a former police officer, tall and muscular. Man, I must have been so deep in the closet that I hadn't yet developed my gaydar (gay radar – we all have it) – how could I not see that??? All joking aside, I feel like he was one of my first angels. He was presented to me at the right time. I cannot overstate how important he was to me when I first blurted out that I was gay – he was a pseudo-therapist. It was great to finally talk to someone about my disturbing life at home. The benefit was two-fold – I was getting things off my chest and I was gaining the perspective of a neutral party. What I didn't realize was that my life was completely toxic, my thinking was all wrong. Like the Geico commercial said, 'that's not how it works, that's not how any of this works.'

He turned into my 'how to be gay' therapist. I started this chapter about needing a gay playbook and I wasn't kidding. I knew nothing about going to bars, dating and hook-up apps. Were there gay dads like me? I wasn't nearly as fabulous or flamboyant as I am now. I guess he was my first gay friend. It took me over forty years to find one. I truly expected that gay people would be so dramatically different – it was so easy to think of them as others. But of course, he was real and nice and human. What I didn't realize was that I was the same. Being gay wasn't wrong or foreign. It was just who I was. Meeting him was the first entry into the world that I was meant to be a part of. And once I entered that world, it was like entering the Land of Oz. My black and white existence became color.

I came back to the house a week later to see my children and explain that mom and dad were separating. Honestly, I can't recall what was said at the time. I don't even know if I said anything at all – my wife may have done all the talking. Before I came back to the house, there are three things that I distinctly recall:

1. I didn't go to work during that week – I didn't respond to e-mail, calls or texts – I sort of went off the grid. Looking back now, it was a mental health break, an opportunity to reboot. My co-workers didn't understand and I don't blame them. I wasn't in the office and I wasn't on vacation – where the heck was I? What was I doing? All I can say is that the time out saved me – I eventually came back, a happier and freer version of me emerged. I'm sure there were rumors that I had some type of nervous breakdown and maybe I did in a way. Either way – in that cocooning session I went from a straight caterpillar to a rainbow butterfly.
2. My wife and I only communicated via e-mail – my plan was to wait 24 hours to respond to any of her incredibly long-winded messages. I think it was the lack of an immediate response that drove her crazy.
3. I came home to find out the locks had been changed – to MY house – I'm the one that pays the mortgage! I had to call the Sheriff's Department to gain access. She claimed that the keys were lost. Again, it's just another example of the batshit stuff that is thankfully in the past.

It's not fun recalling this, I don't receive any pleasure from it – it's just a part of my past and amazingly it is in the past. When you are caught in a cycle of despair, not only can you not see your way out, but you also perceive that reality as the only reality – the only way to live.

Taking control of my life was a great first step. Starting to become comfortable with myself was a wonderful second step. But this is a journey of many steps – check out the image on the next page, on the left is the last photo of me in the closet vs. 18 months later. That later version of Peter is certainly happier and more confident, but there were still unforeseen obstacles in my future. When you assume control, you are essentially taking power from others. I had to continually fight to create the man that I was becoming. I needed to assume strength that I didn't yet possess. Or maybe I did have the strength, but I let it twist in the wind. The next battle was just around the corner – that's another day, another chapter.

PS – one more addition to the Gay Dictionary. When you are in the car providing driving directions to your LGBTQ+ friend, you never say 'go straight.' You say 'go gayly forward.'

Chapter One-and-a-Half

So…When Did You Know?

When people find out that I came out so late in life, they normally ask me (a) when I knew that I was gay and (b) if I'm bisexual. I'm usually flabbergasted when it comes up in conversation – I'm still rather insecure about it and don't have a clear and concise story plus there's a part of me that's thinking, "well, it's none of your business and it's pretty rude of you to just expect me to expose my biggest weakness to you." Then I say, "calm down Mary, they're just curious. You are unique in that you didn't embrace your true identity for the majority of your adult life. Of course they're going to want to know the story."

I'm not bisexual – I'm only attracted to men and I've always been that way. And yes I was married to a woman for over 20 years. Throughout this story you'll learn a lot about my relationship with her – its beautiful origin, the struggles and triumphs and eventually the sad and tragic end. But of course there's another part of me that was always there. It first existed in high school when I was attracted to beefy guys on television wrestling shows (Google Arn Anderson – what a bear fantasy!) and it remained dormant, it stayed in the background during my 20s and 30s. I sort of knew what it was but I did my best to not think about it, to not feed that part of myself. When I think about how I've changed over the past 9+ years since embracing my true identity, it's easy to see that I'm feeding my soul, I'm NOT starving any part of me that brings me joy. I'm now a full, happy and complete person.

It's easy to play Monday Morning Quarterback and tell that younger Peter to just be himself and not worry about what others may think or say. He shouldn't subject himself to endless anguish and doubt and just live in the moment. I'm sorry to say that it didn't work out for that Peter. Whether it was the decisions he made or friends and family that influenced him or something else that made him scared ALL THE TIME, it wasn't his time. He created a life that upon reflection, was never going to work out. He couldn't foresee a future where he would ever be genuinely happy and showcase his full identity, so he did the next best thing. He needed time to overcome his fear and not settle for a life only half lived.

Glowing Up Gay

The majority of my story does not revolve around the power of my dynamic personality and an inspirational journey of self-actualization. Thankfully my development has a happy ending and an optimistic future, but for many years of my life, I have seen myself as a coward. I do acknowledge that it's brave to come out of the closet at any age and especially after you've created a multi-decade persona, but I see most of my young life as one without taking personal risks and wasting emotional energy to deny who I was and spending most of my time pretending to be one person while the real person was effectively dying inside.

I know this isn't uplifting, it may even be damn depressing to read, but I want to convey the deep depression and self-isolation and just plain loneliness that I was experiencing, day after day. It's not like I was living in a dark room by myself – I had some friends, traveled for work, had children, played sports – I was active. All of those activities were masking my internal sadness, emptiness and most importantly, my self-loathing. At the time I hated Peter with the burning rage of a thousand suns. I hated what was inside of him and how it fucked up the outside part of him that was trying to fit in. I hated that he wasn't a normal straight guy. I hated that he was attracted to bigger guys, not like the few gay characters on television and movies. Most importantly, I hated that he was a liar. Not just an occasional liar, but an everyday one. Everything about him was a fraud, a charade. Whatever happiness he had realized, he didn't deserve it, any accomplishments he achieved, he didn't earn it. The black hole inside of me was a magnet that sucked all of the energy and light out of the room; it was an anchor. I felt like I was wearing an invisible black shroud that represented death. I felt ugly on the inside, like I was rotting or some type of metaphorical stench was emanating from me.

If I'm being honest with myself, I've always known that I was gay and for most of my life, I punished myself for being that way. I can't go back in time and live a different life, presumably a better one. I chose to fit into a world that didn't exactly suit me and sadly, I made Peter's life miserable through the choices he made. In many ways my eventual coming out process was about embracing and fully loving all parts of me and most importantly, forgiving young Peter. I had to reconcile my previous struggles and not let them hold me down. My coming out metamorphosis was as much shredding, eliminating and 'un-learning' the old me while simultaneously creating a new me. That's why it's such a curious journey of discovery.

Serious face, serious hair.

Chapter Two

October 1987 – It Was A Tragic Love Story

This was not the life I envisioned for myself when I met my future wife in college. She was one of the first 10 people that I met, as she and her roommate assisted new students. We chatted, connected, and went back to their dorm and drank something trendy like wine coolers. Wow, college was going to rock! Maybe I would have my first girlfriend and be like everyone else. Our first meeting was eventful, but I didn't see her again for a year – we lived in separate parts of the campus and she later admitted that I was "too nice to date."

As fate would have it, she became a Resident Assistant and moved upstairs. It was meant to be! I saw her again and was mesmerized. Reconnecting with her was exhilarating – she was everything I wanted in a woman: smart, pretty and Irish Catholic, which would make my mother happy. She was also studying psychology, just like me. By October we were dating – our connection was instant and our attraction for each other was palpable. We were inseparable for the next three years. I finally had my girlfriend and convinced myself that I was just like everyone else and found someone to build a life with. We shared the same values on wanting children, furthering our education and desire to relocate. The relationship was easy. Of course we did fight - she's half Italian and half Irish – what a temper! However, we grew up together and developed into a happy, loving couple. Before we had children we had many years of fun, romance and bliss.

My college experience was pretty fantastic in many ways: I was an excellent student with beautiful sandy blonde hair, had a pretty and smart girlfriend; my future looked bright. At the time I wanted to become a psychologist, I had a passion for helping others. Later I became the president of the school Psychology Club and then a Resident Assistant – I had leadership potential. I was solely focused on my studies and my girlfriend. I didn't go out to bars or parties. Flash forward to the future – my children in high school are only focused on their studies – no social life, no clubs or sports – pretty much school, family and home.

Sometimes I wonder what my wife saw in me. While we were similar in many ways and there's a comfort in familiarity, I wasn't a typical guy. If you look at who I was at the time, my guess is that I was a safe choice. I like playing and watching sports but I'm not particularly aggressive or masculine. I don't drink beer, not into cars and didn't look at other women. I was also a newbie with relationships. I didn't date in high school, so I married the first and only girl I ever kissed.

I recognize that when you fall in love and get married in your 20's, you haven't truly figured out who you are and what you like - you're still very much a product of your upbringing – will you marry a woman who's like your mother (I did – yikes!) or devote your life to a guy who's nothing like your father (my wife did). But life was fun and easy and I was doing what I wanted and what was expected of me: complete my education, meet a nice Catholic girl and get married in the church. Just be a nice (straight) Catholic boy.

We were the first of my friends to tie the knot, in June 1993. We were young and in love and ready to start a family. We were living in Boston as she was finishing her Masters in Social Work degree. Within a year we would move to North Carolina as I received my MBA in marketing.

Our life was uncomplicated. We had a plan – it was education first then start having kids, hopefully one boy and one girl. I wanted to have children with this woman and I was truly in love with her. Yes, I knew I was hiding a secret, but I didn't want to miss out on becoming a parent.

Having children turned out to be rather arduous. At the time, we were told that when you are trying to get pregnant during the right time each month, it's about 25% successful. It didn't work for us in the first or the second month or any month over the next year. We had a problem and needed answers. We started with my wife, assuming it was some type of ovulation-related issue. Guess what – it wasn't – she was working just fine. The next step focused on me with a sperm test – was I producing enough sperm? Were my boys good swimmers?

The shocking answers to both questions were no and no. I learned over the phone from the doctor's nurse that I wasn't able to have children. They told me that my sperm count was zero and nothing else. Their "customer care" was severely lacking in care - they didn't console me or suggest alternatives. When you learn something like this about yourself it wounds your pride. Instinctually when you can't produce, I would argue that you feel less of a man.

As I stated earlier, we had a plan –so now we commenced with Plan B, finding a sperm donor. I'll note later that my wife and I had an aligned "matter-of-fact" attitude when it came to achieving a goal. If the first plan doesn't work, you figure out another plan and go with that one. I'll always be grateful for the way that she would stick with something, that she wouldn't give up. Along the same vein, there was never any question that I was (and still am!) the children's father. We were in sync at the time, but things will eventually change – remember that the title of this chapter is TRAGIC love story.

Speaking of our story, we found a sperm bank and went shopping for men. Literally we went through a catalog and looked at their height, weight, education and ethnicity. We decided on a medical student who was taller than me and played multiple instruments. He was 'our guy' – we purchased multiple vials as we planned to have two children and they would have the same biological mother and father. From what we knew, we liked what we read about him. Later we purchased an audio recording of him talking about his upbringing and his family (basic background questions, nothing personal). He spoke for about five or six minutes and I was pleased as punch – I liked his voice! He sounded like a great guy! We felt like he had made a great choice.

We quickly became pregnant and all was well in our world. The pregnancy was developing smoothly and we were about to embark on a new life in Florida. It was all about new beginnings for me, personally and professionally. I look back on the innocence of that time with a weird combination of sentimentality and heartbreak – it was a good life, we seemed to have everything you would want out of life…before all the shit went down.

Chapter Three

October 2000 - A Heartbreak, The Miracle, My Greatest Accomplishment

You would think that coming out of the closet in your 40s and rediscovering yourself and what makes you happy would be my greatest personal triumph. As much as I am ecstatic about my life, my love and my support system, my greatest accomplishment involves a tremendous amount of perseverance from my wife – she rightfully deserves most of the credit for helping my son overcome a childhood illness. It wasn't easy – we spent many years visiting doctors across the country trying to identify and help our son recover and it worked – we were lucky.

The pregnancy that I mentioned in the previous chapter did not work out. Unfortunately, that baby suffered from a fatal birth defect, anencephaly. It was explained to us that the baby's spinal cord did not form correctly, thus the baby did not have a frontal lobe. We were on the road to becoming new parents and didn't know anyone who had suffered anything like this. Two things helped us recover over time: my boss gave us the book <u>When Bad Things Happen to Good People</u> and a support group for parents with similar issues. The group sessions reminded us that we weren't alone, that other young couples would listen to our story and share their heartbreaks and triumphs.

That baby died in October 1999 and thankfully, we quickly got pregnant again and our son was born in October of the following year. To say that my wife was nervous this time around would be a major understatement. It was important for her to take extra Folic Acid and I remember that Blue Cross was particularly supportive as she was now considered a high-risk pregnancy.

Everything progressed normally, but we did pass the due date. The doctor decided that she would be induced on a Monday. We were all set to have a fun yet relaxing weekend – go to the movies, visit restaurants, all the things you can enjoy before your parental responsibilities click in. Around 7:00 am on Friday, she woke up with heartburn and stated that she felt something in her stomach about every 10 minutes – she thought it was her Mexican dinner from the night before. I wish I could accurately describe her puzzled face as she pleaded, "do you think it's gas?" I responded, "no silly, you're having a baby." Our son was born just over seven hours later, and he was gorgeous from the minute he entered the world. Happy and calm, it was like we could finally relax — we finally had a beautiful boy.

I should have said BIG boy — he was 7-8 pounds at birth and with every check-up he kept growing, he was at the 99% percentile in height and weight at every doctor's visit. At one year old, before our major setback, he was 30 pounds. I realize now that this is not typical — but he was the only baby I had ever raised — wasn't every kid this way?

What I'm going to share next is controversial. It is not widely accepted, technically there is no scientific proof. All I can say is that my child endured some major setbacks in his development and my wife and I enlisted the help of doctors from various disciplines to help our son recover, full stop. This story is not about advocating a certain medical practice. I'm only sharing my experiences with MY child and the decisions that WE made to help him become the young man that he is today. Frankly, I don't care if you don't believe this portion of the story or not, but I'm thankful for the choices that we made and the chances that we took.

I believe that as a result of the MMR vaccine, my son developed Autism-like symptoms. I know it sounds crazy; it screams anti-science. I am not an anti-vaxxer - I'm vaccinated against COVID-19 and I don't believe in conspiracy theories. All I can say is that when my son came home from his twelve-month check-up, he wasn't the same child. All developmental milestones stopped and in many instances, he regressed. The first thing that we noticed was his inability to eat solid foods — he could not progress past Stage 2 baby food — anything chunkier would make him gag. We thought it was something about his throat, some type of inability to swallow. Then his diet became more and more limited — within a few months, he only wanted milk, potato chips, French Fries, and pancakes from our local First Watch restaurant. We would later beg the restaurant for prepared mix, telling them that was the only thing he would eat and thankfully, they helped us out.

At some point we realized that he was no longer talking. He said a few words before his doctor's appointment, but now nothing. He would essentially be silent for the next 18 months. We also checked his hearing

— he wasn't paying attention to us and didn't seem to notice us. Then came letters and numbers — that was his 'thing.' You have probably heard that children on the Autism spectrum can focus on repetitive activities or they may have a hyper-focused hobby or interest. Letters and numbers made him happy — he looked at them, arranged them and smiled as he played with them. If there was another person in the room or if a Baby Einstein video was playing, it didn't matter. It's like we were invisible to him.

When you have a kid, people usually ask how they are doing — it's the polite thing to do, plus it's almost always good news. You don't want to bring people down with your story of some type of unknown condition that you think your kid may have, but you don't know, you're still figuring it out. I remember coining a phrase, "there's nothing wrong with our son, but something's not right."

We didn't know anyone who was dealing with anything like this — it was a confusing and stressful time. One weekend we tried to get our mind off things and we went to the movies — we saw "Signs" with Mel Gibson. He plays a preacher who has lost his faith and at the end of the movie his son nearly dies. He rediscovers his faith when he's asking God for his son to be saved - it's the pivotal scene and the emotional center of the film. We leave the theater, get into our car, and I break down; tears are flowing from everywhere and I can't stop crying, I can't catch my breath. After 15-20 minutes of sobbing, I plead to my wife that our son is so fragile, saying the last word in about four syllables. He was nearly two years old and we were so lost, that we saw no future for him. We wanted to have faith like the movie, but the outlook was dim.

Our lives changed forever, and my son's recovery path started with a call one night from a Canadian sportswriter. His child had a similar condition and he said, "get your kid off milk." We didn't know what to think, but we were jointly driven by helping our son get better. We always believed that other people must have learned something — we were always willing to try the latest breakthrough, see if it works for us, then move on to the next idea / latest therapy.

At night my wife was an internet sleuth — combing various websites and chatrooms and reaching out to doctors or therapists, trying to find someone who could help our son, anyone who could explain what was going on. She spent hours pouring her heart out and sharing our story. She was passionate, determined, driven and successful. Numerous times we were able to get doctors on the phone and sometimes we were able to get on their schedule, flying to Washington D.C. or Los Angeles to see the latest therapy or treatment.

I said that we shared a similar philosophy of learning, implement, then go learn again. It's a fair question to ask why we were so sure that we could 'recover' our son? Aren't children born with Autism? Again, I'm not going to argue how and when children are on the Autism spectrum – we believed that our son was damaged by vaccines and that through perseverance and maybe a little luck, we could reverse that damage. Why did we believe that? Because over time, we observed that his symptoms were inconsistent. In the winter when he would have strep throat or something similar, his condition would disappear. It was an awesome 24-48-hour miracle; our happy-go-lucky son had returned to us! There is a theory that children that are vaccine damaged are suffering from inflammation and/or an immune system response, and that when responding to an illness, it temporarily suppresses that condition. There was also a reverse situation – if our son did not poop for 1-2 days, his symptoms would be worse and he would be hyperactive. Again, we did not start with this thinking – this was a learn-as-you-go plan. Through trial and error, we figured out what worked with our son. To get him healthy, to get him back, it required a full-court press of diet AND supplements AND physical and occupational therapy.

Switching my son from cow's milk to rice milk produced almost immediate results. I mentioned that milk was one of the few things he enjoyed - he was drinking 8-9 glasses a day! The first amazing benefit occurred about three weeks later – he no longer had a glassy look in his eyes, it was like he was seeing us and interacting with us for the first time in months. Remember that he was still non-verbal. Soon after the milk switcheroo there was a cartoon on the television and a mouse was going down a slide, he had seen it plenty of times. Suddenly, he starts patting his chest, almost pointing to himself. We weren't sure at first, but we realized that he was communicating that HE had a slide in his backyard.

There were so many things amazing with that one gesture – he was aware AND talking about himself AND he wanted to communicate with us!

The idea that our son was in there the whole time, that he was somewhere trapped inside and that we were helping him out, was so encouraging. It was progress. There was also one small yet significant milestone – it was around Christmas and we weren't particularly joyful that year. When you have a two-year-old child that doesn't interact with you, doesn't want toys, and is pretty much unaware of Santa and people in general, the holiday doesn't mean much. We were having pork chops and we cut up some small bites and put them on his highchair tray. Every night the solid food just sat there but this night, this Christmas miracle, he picked up one, put it in his mouth, chewed and swallowed. It really happened!

He finally said his first word a few weeks later. It was 'helicopter.' We had been reading to him since birth and apparently, all these words were also inside of him. He went from one to around 300 words in a matter of weeks. It was a verbal explosion! Incredibly, he topped that when he turned three – he started reading. Again, he went from non-verbal to savant within a year. Many children can 'read-ish' books when they're young, but it's really that they've memorized books that they've heard again and again. My boss didn't believe us until our sons went on a playdate together; we stopped at McDonald's and my son said, "McRib is back."

All these achievements were outstanding, and we were blessed (lucky) that our son was improving, that he was developing. But make no mistake, he was not like other kids. He did not play with others; he did not have friends. He was still very much in his own world. We'll never know if it was a situation where he didn't need other kids or if he just never learned how to be with others. While we were ecstatic that he was finally talking, in many ways it was a one-way conversation – he was expressing what he was thinking and feeling, but he didn't necessarily know how to respond and react to others.

We taught him to read facial expressions and how to look for visual cues. Many times, during a conversation he would just stop and ask, 'what are you feeling?' It wasn't natural for him to read what my face was saying and understand if our conversation was engaging (smiling, making eye contact) or if I'm bored (frown, distracted). Another skill that we worked on was how to have a back-and-forth dialogue / how to transition from one topic to another. I mentioned that he could carry on a conversation if it was a subject that interested him. We had to teach him to both listen to the other person as well as share your thoughts. So, when the conversation was not directly about him or what he wanted to share, he would ask us for permission to "create a bridge" to his topic. Helping our son be aware of the world was our second 'silent' job – the world had finally opened to him and we needed to teach him how to participate in it.

There are tons of struggles when you have a child that didn't look or act like other kids. Invitations to birthday parties dry up, playdates are few and far between, and you schedule your day around your child's good vs. bad moods. You arrange your day to present your child in certain situations (i.e., after his nap, before the store gets crowded) so that he will look like a typical child. Much like the struggles that I suffered later in life, our world became small – we were alone. It was the online community – the others like us - who were the only people that understood our situation. We were living in Florida at the time – we left our pediatrician because he didn't support us, and we did not believe that we were receiving adequate services for his disability. We did find one of the best public school systems in the country for children with special needs, it was in Naperville, Illinois. Guess where we moved in 2004!

Before I share our Chicagoland stories, I should probably mention that around the same time that my son was finally 'present,' we welcomed his baby sister. We always knew that we wanted two kids and were pleased that we had a boy and a girl. The more sobering answer was that at the time when we became pregnant with our daughter, we didn't know if our son was ever going to get better. We had no earthly idea of whether he would be able to live on his own. Could he get a job? Could he be in any kind of relationship? When you are a parent of a child with developmental difficulties, your number one fear is dying. Our life centered around a daily routine of helping him navigate the world and we knew all the ways to make him happy (it was more like reducing his struggles) – your most precious worry is that someone else can't replicate that.

Our daughter appeared to be typical – happy and healthy. She was born in Florida and moved with the rest of us when she was under a year old. Do you remember those Baby Bjorn baby backpacks? I loved wearing those, especially when she was 5-6 months old. I could walk around, and she would sleep in it and I could smell her perfect fresh-scented head – so intoxicating! Once we took separate flights to O'Hare airport – my wife took our son and I carried our daughter. When you are a single male passenger with a young child, EVERYONE at the airport looks at you and forms an opinion of you. Many people, almost all women, gaze at you with loving eyes, one of those 'awwwww, what a great dad!' looks. However, there's still a substantial number of people who are staring at you a little too long, giving you the side eye. Wanna know what their shifty looks are saying? It was obvious, they were trying to figure out where the baby's mother was, deciding whether I had stolen that baby or not. It was hilarious to be both admired and reviled at the same time!

We lived in Chicago for two years and during our stay we achieved our two primary objectives – our son received special needs services in the public school system, and we were a patient of an alternative medicine doctor. I mentioned before that getting my son off cow's milk was a breakthrough – it was a gluten-free, casein-free diet that helped him, it's what worked for us. To us, his diet played a significant role in his recovery, we were getting his gut healthy. You might think that I'm obsessed with this topic, but I'm going to talk about poop again. Despite the impressive progress that you could see externally, his insides were telling a different story. Simply put, for years his bowel movements smelled like raw sewage, like he was sick on the inside. Again, we don't claim to be medical experts, but we knew that if we wanted our son to reach his full potential, to overcome his earlier struggles, we needed to get this under control. Dare I say, we needed to get our shit together (groan!). A strict diet and specific supplements were our recipe for his health and recovery. Our weekly grocery trips included stops to the Natural Food store to purchase gluten-free bread and waffle mix, as well as buying expensive probiotics, the kind that is refrigerated. If we ever slipped up and gave him something with traces of gluten, we found that digestive enzymes worked for us – he would eventually process it.

Overall, living in Chicago for us was dreadful – I always thought that it was a sign that in the two winters that we lived there, there were two major snowstorms on the day before Thanksgiving. It was like Mother Nature was saying 'BOOM, welcome to winter – it's gonna suck for the next four months!' Have you ever heard that there are two seasons in Chicago? Winter and Construction. Compounding the miserable, non-Florida-like weather was that we didn't make any friends, I didn't like the house that we lived in, I didn't care for my job, and we were a miserable couple. While we were seeing slow progress with our son, our focused efforts were a convenient excuse to not talk about the state of our marriage – we were struggling financially, we didn't particularly like each other, no romance, didn't sleep in the same bed, didn't have sex anymore. We were essentially roommates. I am not laying any blame on my wife – obviously I was struggling with my sexual identity and the fear of being outed.

Between these horrible memories there were pops of wonder and enjoyment – life isn't always all bad or all good. We used to frequent this breakfast diner called Blueberry Hill and when you take children out for breakfast, they primarily want to eat the good stuff – waffles or bacon – but they seldom finish their eggs. It's a struggle to make them eat protein versus fat and sugar. One day I had this crazy idea – my son just finished eating (minus the eggs) and I touched his forehead. I furrow my brow and say, "oh no, your Protein Temperature is low, only 27 percent." He confusingly asks, "how do I get it higher?" I suggest he take a bite of his eggs and again touch his face and declare that he's now at 38 percent. I calmly explain that he'll get to 100 when he completes his meal. The waitress stops by and she's immediately in on the joke, validates what I'm saying, and my son shovels in his food to achieve a perfect score. That trick worked for another 1-2 years and the best part of this vignette is that my children remember it and realized that they were fooled by their father – Parenting Awesomeness level achieved! .

You might be asking why I stayed in the marriage, why didn't I leave. It's a jumble of emotions, fear and responsibility. You already know about my many reservations, but more importantly I had a child with special needs. We had two children, and our daughter was not getting the attention she deserved; improving our son's health was our sole focus.

While I am pleased that I was supporting our family, there was a cost to stay in our loveless relationship. My self-loathing reasoned that my happiness wasn't that important, that if I left it would potentially jeopardize my son's progress and overall health. To repeat, I don't deserve any praise, no one is waiting to hand me a medal. I did what I thought was right to provide for my family, and if I was particularly happy or not, it didn't matter. Helping him recover from his illness is the greatest accomplishment in my life – I would go through the same sufferings all over again if I had to.

In that way I'm just like my father. My parents had two girls and when they were in their early 40s they had a 'happy accident' – triplets! I'm the youngest of the three – the baby of the family. Having three babies upended our family – we moved into a larger home and my mother moved away from her sister, who lived next door. I can imagine that moving and starting anew was a chance for my parents to reinvent themselves, to begin a new chapter. I say this without knowing the truth – my mother valued privacy above all else. It wasn't our business to know what was going on in their relationship, it wasn't right for the neighbors to know what went on in our home behind closed doors.

Chapter Four

1970's – 1980's – Triple-Trouble, Family Die-Namics

My mother knew that she was having twins but didn't learn that she was having triplets until FOUR HOURS before we were born via x-ray, as there were no ultrasounds back then. This pregnancy felt different from the first two, but no one believed her when she said, 'something's not right.' She was also huge – like *National Enquirer* big! At some point her doctor told her to go on a diet of all things and by six months, she couldn't walk anymore and was pretty much bedridden. By the time we were born, she had fourteen pounds of baby in her – I was the largest at almost five pounds. I was in an incubator for three weeks, with my brother and sister for four weeks. My mother, God love her, would share the most horrible details – she said that I looked like a very tiny baby and that my brother and sister both looked like fishes. Yikes! What a way to create a complex!

To this day I don't know how my mother managed the whole mothering thing, pretty much by herself. We had two children in my 30s, three years apart, I was home almost every night, and we still could not have managed another child. My mother had three AT ONE TIME and somehow didn't end up in the looney bin. It was common for us to tell people that our older sisters 'could help,' but you can probably imagine that with the triplets dominating my mother's attention, they must have felt like yesterday's news.

My mother was a stay-at-home mom – she didn't go to college and only had 1-2 secretarial jobs before meeting her husband. When I say, 'at home,' I mean it. My mother COULDN'T leave – she didn't learn to drive until she was fifty years old. This sounds so old school and I guess it is. For my mother, getting her license was a form of independence, dare I say defiance, from her VERY traditional role with her husband. Part of learning to drive is practical – soccer & baseball practices for the triplets, etc., but I'm sure my mother also saw it as an opportunity to define herself outside of 'Mrs. Paul Leahy.'

My childhood was not bad, not even close. I don't remember that we were any different from our community – we had what we needed: food, clothes and toys and stuff. We weren't rich, but we didn't struggle as far as I could tell, we had little-to-no debt outside of the mortgage. I wasn't lacking for friends or things to do, outside or inside the house – only four minutes separated my brother and me and we were pretty much inseparable 24/7. Our neighborhood was littered with kids of all ages and we lived in a safe town – I could ride my bike anywhere. We were always outside – sports ruled our daily lives, always playing basketball, street hockey, soccer and stickball. I can even remember games like "Ghost in the Calaboose," sort of a team hide and go seek, perfect for warm summer nights.

My mother was extremely proud of raising triplets – she always felt that this accomplishment, and the triumphs and struggles associated with it, was her ticket into heaven. I 'think' that my father liked working and providing for his family, but the truth is that I don't know, I'll never know. I wholeheartedly believe that both my father and mother were unhappy with their life and partner but had no desire to change or were afraid of leaving what was familiar to them.

My parents had a clear division of responsibility – my father made the money, in fact he worked two jobs for most of our childhood. We normally saw him most weekday mornings before he left for job #1, then we'd see him on the weekend, up early both Saturday and Sunday. His primary job was as a tax auditor and his daily schedule was 8:00 am to 4:00 pm. He would then drive to the beach and take a nap in his car, then go to job #2, working in the money room at a greyhound dog track from 6:00 pm to 11:00 pm. His night would end with his hour-long commute home. He'd be up at 6:00 am to do it all over again. I never heard him complain about working both jobs and he hardly ever got sick (his secret – drinking prune juice every morning). He was the provider and that's how he supported his family, that's how he showed love. In nearly every other way possible, my father was not affectionate to his wife or children. I never saw my parents kiss and I can't recall either of them ever paying a compliment to their spouse.

My mother's responsibility was the children and the home, she was both the father and the mother Monday through Friday. She pretty much had the weekend too. My dad was around for those two days, but my mom still ran the show. Again, I'll never know their motivations – my mother didn't usually 'hand' the triplets to her husband on Saturday so that she could take a break. Similarly, my dad wasn't 'itching' to spend quality time with the kiddos.

There's a famous story in our family…one snowy Saturday in January, my mother needed a break. She took the bus into Boston for shopping and to be free of the kids for a few hours. She knew that managing the kids was an all-day affair – putting on snow pants and jackets, taking them off when someone invariably needed the bathroom, whiny kids asking for a snack or cocoa, the whole shebang. While she was happy to get away, there was a part of her that wanted my father to experience her life for just an afternoon, how she was always on call. She walked in the door, shopping bags draped across both arms, and the house was quiet, my father in the family room reading the newspaper. Perplexed, she asked him, 'how was your day? How were the kids? Was it a struggle to get them in and out of their clothes? He looked up from the paper and said, "I don't know, I helped them get ready to go outside, then I locked the door."

From the outside we looked like a typical family – we were no better, no worse than anyone else. Whether it was unconscious or on purpose, my parents had favorites – my dad chose my brother and my older sister, and my mom chose me and my oldest sister. Remember that there were five children, so one was definitely on the outside looking in. That's fucked up and cruel and a lot of rejection/lack of affection going on.

I was fortunate to be one of my mother's favorites – remember, she ran the household. She claimed ignorance, but it was no secret who she preferred. I was always her 'can do no wrong' child and my triplet brother and sister were constantly overcoming her biases and negative assumptions. It was unfair to them and it made them incredibly jealous of me. But of course, every light includes some dark. My father ignored me and at some point (age 13?) he wrote me off. He decided that since I belonged to his wife, I was now invisible to him. While I am secure and love myself because of how my mother supported me, I still have buried bruises from my father's abandonment.

When I was in high school I wrote my father a letter, asking him if he loved me. He never acknowledged it; I don't know if he read it. My mother did and tried to engage him, but nothing happened. She could see my hurt and was even more nurturing, which played out just like you think – my mom loved me even more and my father cared about me even less. When I met some of my friend's fathers, I instantly hated them. If there was any joke or gentle ribbing about their son, I took it personally, I was red with anger. Well, you don't need to be a college freshman psychology major to see what's going on there. I was jealous, I was hurt; I wanted a father. Any negative feelings toward these guys were a wish that I had someone like that in my life.

In college I had a big revelation about my parents – my older sisters had come to the same conclusion around the same age. My family dynamics hadn't changed, I was forever my mother's son. However, with a little time away, you see your parents in a different light, that the story that you've always believed isn't necessarily the whole truth. We were with our mother nearly all the time and of course you're going to favor her by default, you're going to believe that she's telling you the truth. But my mom was human and as I mentioned, she didn't particularly care for her husband. She had the power at home and the children's ear, and we were taught to hate our father, to only see his negative qualities or the things that he didn't do for the family. It was an eye-opener to see my mom from his perspective, that she wasn't always a walk in the park and that he did not receive the credit for his dedication to the family. That he might have been unhappy and/or stuck in a marriage in which he wasn't supported. Spoiler Alert: I replicated this EXACT situation with my wife and our children – I could kick myself for letting history repeat itself!

When I first met my wife, I cried a lot over my father. She was my therapist, helping me deal with his rejection, convincing me that I was good enough and deserving of love. There was never any resolution with him, we all just moved on. He had his favorites and my heart grew into a stone for him. Maybe I did it to protect myself, maybe I did it because I was still angry. When I had children, I vowed that I would be different. I would be demonstrative, I would be affectionate, I would be present.

Two episodes that cemented our fractured relationship have always stuck with me. I was living in Florida and a tax auditor was working temporarily in our office, he was an older gentleman. I happen to strike up a conversation with him and could immediately detect his Boston accent and I asked him where he lived in Mass. After 5-10 minutes I learned that he worked the same job up north when he was younger, before he semi-retired to the Sunshine State. Within another 5-10 minutes we learned that he worked WITH my dad, he knew him! I peppered him with questions – what was he like? What do you remember about him? I was interrogating him like my dad was a long-lost relative. While I knew some of his hobbies, I never knew him as a person – what made him tick, what were his passions.

Armed with this treasure trove of details, I excitedly told my wife that I was going to call home and share this great news with my dad. We never spoke, I was not 'his' child. Every time I phoned, if he picked up he would say the same thing, "let me get your mother." This time it was going to be different - I met someone he knew, I had great information to share and he HAD to speak to me this time! And just like Charlie Brown with Lucy Van Pelt and the football, I fell for it. Once I told him who I met at work, he stated, "that's great" and put the phone down, leaving me in silence until my mother picked it back up to continue the conversation. Just like the Peanuts cartoon, I ran as fast as I could, got my hopes up that we would have something to talk about (aka, kick the ball), only to fall flat on my back.

The second one sprung from a science fiction movie from 2000 called "Frequency" with Jim Caviezel and Dennis Quaid. A man uses a ham radio one night in the present during the aurora borealis and he ends up talking to his father in 1969, just before he dies. Within major themes about redemption, making up for lost time and rekindling a lost father-son relationship, I was an emotional wreck at the end of the show. I wanted my life to be like the movie, I wanted a happy ending. I just wanted my father to love me. It was crushing to never receive any acknowledgments from him. I was a great student in college and I got married in the church to a nice Catholic girl. What more could I have done to please him, for him to even notice me? At one point I called home and told him about the movie and how it impacted me. To his credit he wanted to talk about my feelings, but I said no. I said, 'Dad, it's too late.' I couldn't take the chance that he did want to truly connect with me. He was over 75 years old at the time and maybe he had regrets, but I couldn't risk it. He didn't push it and I didn't allow myself to ever be vulnerable again. We never spoke after that call and within a few years he was dead. I never heard him say 'I love you son.'

The second paragraph of this book simply states the critical emotional issue of my adult life and the eventual breakthrough – I decided to be in the closet for over forty years. My awkward relationship with my father plays a part in this decision to not be myself, the fear of being in his eyes 'a damn fag.' Was it a fear of disappointing him? Of course it was. I wasn't secure enough to be proud of who I was with him and now it's too late – he died 10 years before I finally came to terms with my sexual identity. It might be my greatest disappointment that my father never got to see the real me.

It's not exactly about being myself. I would love to tell him that my marriage was just like his – I was miserable, I was underappreciated. But I got out – somehow, I fucking did it. I didn't want to be a whiny baby who was stuck and not in control of his life. Maybe I could have told him that I truly understood how he suffered, how he was a great family provider and he passed on that quality and I played that role in my family. I would also love to tell him how sorry I was to play a part in the fight with his wife – that she made him the enemy of his children for most of their formative years.

Most importantly, I would want him to be at peace, to know that I'm now quite happy. The cycle of settling for an unhappy marriage had been broken.

OF COURSE I'm the one on the right, drawing attention to himself

Chapter Five

A timeless story - Family Lost, Family Found

I am not particularly close to my family – it's up there as one of my biggest regrets. I've spent more than half my life living away from my hometown. I consider myself a Bostonian but with many moves, I don't have a place that I can realistically call my home. If I had the chance to go back in time, I would have never left Massachusetts. I cannot say that I would now have some idyllic family life and that I would be bonded to my sisters and my cousins, my kids would know their kids, etc. But I moved away and didn't establish any type of connections or family traditions, so there's no history there. At this point we only get to see a large portion of our family at a wedding or a funeral. It's been over seven years that my four siblings and I were together, when we buried my mother. It was then, in the town where I grew up, that I felt like I didn't belong there anymore – I've been away for over twenty-five years. Again, this broke my heart. Can you ever go home again?

After college I moved all over the country for various reasons (graduate school, jobs). I just did the math, I had eleven different addresses over thirty-two years. Just using state abbreviations is exhausting: MA to CA to MA to NC to KS to MO to FL to IL to GA to CA. Even now, many of my high school friends have asked me for my address multiple times, they are used to my transitory life.

Those individual moves made sense at the time, but I feel that I missed the opportunity to establish roots and have a legacy in a community. As I grow older, that's what is important now, it's having real, genuine relationships with lots of shared histories. Those many moves also masked two glaring holes in my life at the time – no lasting friendships and poor budgeting. I mentioned earlier that we were not great at maintaining relationships – the stark reality is that it's easy to move, to start over in another state, if there's not a robust base of friends that want you to stay. After we purchased our first home in Kansas City, these moves also provided a financial benefit. Our secret was that we were always living beyond our means, racking up credit card debt, and by gaining some equity with each home sale, we would rescue ourselves and pay off outstanding balances and start accumulating new debt. Of course, this also meant that the earned equity never accumulated over time and when the housing market crashed in 2008, I couldn't rely on that false sense of unearned wealth.

I spent twenty-odd years being away from my family, making few meaningful relationships and not living in a community that I could call home. Wow – doesn't that sound fun! That was my existence when I left my wife and started over. I had to reinvent myself, but how does one start that? Quoting Indiana Jones, "I don't know, I'm making this up as I go." Over time I created a Chosen Family – people that became part of my tribe, helping me grow. The concept of a Chosen Family has been around for decades within the LGBTQ+ community. Many people were rejected by their families and learned to redefine what a family means, how to create loving and supportive relationships with people not related to you, and people with shared experiences. I was fortunate to be 'adopted' for multiple Thanksgivings and Christmases when I first came out. Holidays can be a lonely affair when your traditional family rejects you and the simple act of opening your home to someone less fortunate is the purest form of 'the reason for the season.'

My Chosen Family evolved as I did, but for me there was one constant, my work wife Joy. Her love for me is unwavering, her support is brutally honest and her disdain for my ex-wife is relentless. She'll kill me for typing this, but she almost asked me out when my wife and I separated. Luckily I quickly shared my 'I'm into guys' announcement and we avoided any awkward conversations.

She was the perfect person in my life, another angel presented to me when I needed to take the next step. Through a weird quirk at our company, she only lived in Georgia for six months, at the exact time that I was embarking on my journey. We both believe that there must have been some type of higher power, a force that bonded us, that she was put there to make me into a whole confident man, to showcase my fabulosity. She is my number one – although we no longer work together and I may have other female BFFs, she will always be my only work wife.

Joy is strong and smart. She started as an engineer in my company and held various roles in sales, training and managing a sales region before starting a successful coaching and consulting career. She uses the word "unapologetic" a lot and it took me some time to understand what she meant. It doesn't mean unyielding; it means not contorting yourself to make someone else comfortable. She "keeps it real" (her words, not mine!) She opened my eyes that my wife was a bully and that because I had been beaten down for so long, my distorted thinking was, frankly, batshit crazy. Joy became my life coach, the 'bullshit detector' for my soon-to-be ex-wife and my fashion consultant. I'll never forget going to Men's Warehouse together and buying a three-piece suit for work, with new shirts, ties, and shoes. I had never spent that kind of money on myself – it was uplifting to look good, feel good, to start to like myself.

Another thing that Joy was always good at – listening to me. She was there when I made my first forays into the gay dating scene, she always had time to listen to my stories, laugh with me at my escapades and be excited for me when I made small leaps of faith. Do you know how rare it is for someone to be genuinely excited about something as small as "I bought a pink tie and pocket square today and I'm going to wear it to work?!"

Joy physically held my hand as I came out to our VP at work. I remember the look on his face – he had been my mentor for years, but we had never been this close personally. In retrospect, I don't think he would have judged me harshly, but it is an example of how very isolated I felt when I was in the closet – I couldn't even let myself trust my mentor at work. It was an emotionally charged moment and I don't know if I would have done it (at least not that soon) had she not pushed me and then supported me.

Joy also met my children a couple of times and I was thrilled that my daughter could see, and potentially learn from, an educated female professional. Anything to promote girl power! She also met my bear friends – it was natural, she was cool and they loved her (huge comic book nerd, loves video games, instantly she was one of the guys) and she was smart and quick with trivia, so I loved having her with us at Team Trivia. She once joked to me that she finally realized why I liked to cuddle with her – she was my "girl bear".

On more than one occasion, Joy was my "mom." She had put down the hammer with me once when I was slightly obsessed with this guy who was my first crush. He lived in Nashville and had just invited me to spend the weekend with him and attend his birthday party that he was hosting. During the previous six months he and I had been chatting and texting. It made me feel good, but realistically, it was a one-way conversation. He wasn't truly interested in me but I perceived the invitation as a breakthrough, that somehow this was his way of wanting to get to know me. I was certain that he wanted a relationship with me - maybe I would finally have my first boyfriend! Reality check - many people were invited to the party and I was just another person to make the party larger, for him to receive even more adulation that night. I wasn't 'special' to him – not then, not ever. As I was gushing about my 'soon-to-be-future-boyfriend,' Joy calmly and firmly stated "you're not going…nothing good can come from it." I pleaded, trying to convince her that I wasn't delusional. She realized before I did that I was ignoring some glaring red flags. Net-net, she won, I lost. I learned a valuable lesson about chasing people and that when you are interested in someone and they reciprocate, you know the difference. It's easy to laugh at my naivete and wishful thinking. I WANTED him to like me and convinced myself that he felt the same way.

I'm putting words in her mouth, but Joy is pretty damn proud of me – how I've grown, how far I've come. I'd rather flip the script and give her all the credit. She was patient when I was a lost soul then let her baby bird fly when he had grown into his 'rainbow wings.' She will always hold a special place in my heart – she knew the miserable me that was in the closet and the real me that is finally happy.

At the risk of demonizing my ex-wife, she met Joy only once and predictably, it was weird and disappointing. I was living in my first apartment and one Saturday Joy and I were on the couch watching a movie. My wife knocked on the door and I let her in. She was surprised that I was not alone and made a subtle, but unmistakable look of shock when she discovered that Joy was black. My wife made sure to complement Joy when she was there and texted me later with effusive praise. But true to her form, during one of our post-separation / pre-divorce fights, she stated that "it's better for you to date a white guy than a black woman." Such a class act – what a pillar of tolerance. I told Joy about this later and she wasn't in the least bit surprised – a sad affair all around.

PS – I am a collage queen – I love mashing-up memories!

This would foreshadow my ex-wife's metamorphosis. As I grew into the man I was meant to be, she devolved from the person that I once knew and loved. Conspiracy theories and twisted personal belief systems became part of her future identity.

Chapter Six

March to June, 2014 – Let's Combine a Divorce AND a Bankruptcy AND another lawsuit

My wife and I had major money problems – we lived beyond our means and used credit cards to make us appear more successful or wealthy or happy. Our debt was a symptom of our larger problems and filing for bankruptcy in 2010 was the best solution for our family. We owed over $100K across various credit cards and vehicles and we were never going to pay that off. That stress was compounded by the constant phone calls from creditors. With Caller ID, we could see who was calling us and the visible stress on our faces as we saw the creditor's phone numbers was scaring the children.

Because of our combined income, the bankruptcy debt was not reduced – there was a set amount ($3,100.00) that was garnished from my paycheck. Like many parts of my life, I wanted this to be kept under wraps, for no one to know my secret. I remember visiting HR a couple of years later when we were issued new corporate credit cards and saying, "um…I don't think mine is going to work anytime soon!"

After my mental health break, I returned to work and needed an apartment. My wife found a place near the children's school and we had enough excess furniture to furnish it. I didn't ask for much, but I did want the king-sized bed. She agreed to it, then said no, then said yes, then reversed again. Finally, I looked at her and said, "I'm going to need the big bed," with the understanding that I wouldn't always be sleeping alone. Putting it that way, she relented quickly. About six months later, the infamous 'Snowmageddon' incident happened in Atlanta (ironically, the day we filed for an uncontested divorce in court) and through a weird twist, I slept that night in our old home with the dog, and she, my children and another elementary school teacher stayed in my apartment. Supposedly my daughter was searching for hair conditioner and looked under the sink and found personal lubricant. Apparently, there was even more snooping and my ex-wife found condoms and sarcastically 'congratulated' me for using personal protection.

BTW, after I signed the lease, she asked for a set of my apartment keys, for emergencies. I said no and she was put off, saying "why are you making this an issue." She didn't win out, but it still amazes me that that was a typical conversation between us, that I was constantly arguing against basic logic or what many would perceive as atypical behavior. Our dynamic was screwed up, our everyday thinking was warped. After I moved in, she asked me to return to the home, twice. On both occasions, it was about the money that we were wasting on my apartment rental, and that we should be spending that money on the children.

One of those requests to come back to the house was included in one of those 'we need to talk' conversations. She came prepared to discuss our money situation, she wanted me to break my apartment lease. She presented a revised household budget - I use the word 'budget' very loosely because it was a Microsoft Word document with categories and estimated spending. Developing a pseudo-budget was a nearly annual event when we were together. We would identify how and where we would spend our money (again, not on a spreadsheet!), but then we would never track anything or adjust the budget if we were overspent on discretionary spending. It's just a wasted effort if you don't track or adjust or hold yourself accountable.

This budget proposal (which I still own, it's in my safe) included the very weird and highly offensive "$1000/month lifestyle budget for Peter." I have no idea what that was, what she was thinking, but I had a hissy fit when I saw that. Again, it screamed that this was my 'gay allowance' or that I received some type of stipend that allowed me to be gay. I immediately stormed out of the Starbucks – it made me feel cheap or less than a real man. Of course, years later I had the perfect comeback – "honey, if you think I need to pay for sex, think again!"

My divorce was chock full of drama. We decided to remain separated for the remainder of that year and finish the year married, for tax purposes. When we had the divorce discussion in January 2014, she suggested that we do it online, as to not waste money on lawyers. She said, "we already agree on everything, we could log in and fill out a form together." Luckily, I didn't entertain this, not for a minute. I needed a lawyer, a GAY one, who was going to do right by me. I lucked out with Steven. Like many of my angels that supported me in my reawakening, he fought for me, backed me, and at least once yelled at me to get my head out of my ass.

The process of negotiating the divorce was not particularly fun – it never is, but we eventually settled on terms - I agreed to eight years of child support and alimony. People will argue that it's too much (my lawyer) or not enough (my wife), but the truth is that this is what I agreed to. I gave what I thought was a generous amount – at the time, the amount that I provided to her each month was more than her take-home pay.

After filing in court, the uncontested divorce process in Georgia is standardized – take an online class on parenting and come back to court in 30-45 days. Around 30 days after the filing (cue ominous background music), I received another 'we need to talk' request. She presented ANOTHER binder/budget scenario and pitched me the idea that after her alimony and child support run out, she would be penniless. She believed that she needed another master's degree (she already had two) to boost her income. Her two-part proposal was:

- ✓ Give her $30,000 now for her third master's degree
- ✓ Agree to the following terms – if, at the end of the alimony and child support, she was not making enough money to have a take-home salary of at least $50,000 annually, I would agree to pay alimony for the rest of my life

Yes, this happened and admittedly it's damn ballsy! I called my lawyer in a semi-panic and he came up with a clever idea: a week before our scheduled court date, he petitioned the court for a quick judgment, and the judge agreed. So, I was able to get the judge to sign off on our divorce terms about six days before our day in court. The next weekend was a wild ride of emotions:

- FRIDAY – I visit her classroom and tell her that she doesn't need to go to court on Monday because our divorce was final earlier in the week. She was apoplectic and called me later that night saying "I see what you and your lawyer did, don't worry I can still sue you. And on Monday I'm going to see the bankruptcy judge and tell her that you cheated on that application, that you've been hiding money. The bankruptcy will be thrown out and you'll have to start over!" I didn't cheat or lie, and I finally got some moxie, knowing that she was just making up shit. I stood up to her (finally) and said, "honey, the less I make, the less you get!"

- SATURDAY – we receive a surprise letter from the bankruptcy judge – our debt will be paid in full next month. This came as a shock to both of us – we thought we had another 11 months on the bankruptcy – we included that anticipated date in our divorce papers. I was dumbfounded that it would be complete in four years – I thought we were on a five-year plan. She did not see it this way and was furious – she believed that I had deceived her and that I knew this was coming. To her, it was unfair that I now had an incremental $3100 a month, she felt that she was entitled to that money.

I came to the house and she was angrily screaming until she suddenly stopped – she had a revelation. "Peter, don't you see? This solves all of our problems! You can just give me $3100 a month for the next year and I can use that money on the children. It's not like you're going to miss the money, you were already paying the bankruptcy." As God as my witness, I seriously considered it and called my lawyer and asked for his opinion. He was the second person to scream at me that day, angrily reminding me that I had no obligation to give her any of the money. He finally said nine simple words that brought me back to reality…" Peter, why do you think you've done something wrong?" It was the simple question that I needed to ask myself. I was still punishing myself for being gay, feeling guilty for getting divorced, and using money to forgive myself for being in the closet for so long. I left and told her that I wasn't going to decide right now.

SUNDAY– I tell her that I am not changing the terms of the divorce. She countered with a request for half of the money for the next 11 months, and that she would not petition the bankruptcy because "it wouldn't be good for the children."

Monday comes and she went to court, I did not. Later that week I received a letter from the judge – he stated that she presented many theories but no facts – to come back if she has actual evidence. Of course, that letter was satisfying to me – you can't just make up facts and ask a judge to believe them.

Like a zombie in a horror movie, this divorce is hard to kill! A few weeks later, she found a Merrill Lynch statement that referenced some stock options that we owned and the number "45.000." The point zero is important – it represents the $45.000 share price (we had about $5,000 total), but she thought I had $45,000 somewhere hidden and she wanted her share of that money. Within 90 days of the divorce, I was served papers to appear in court again, I was accused of lying and hiding money.

I had A LOT of emotions about this lawsuit – PISSED that she thought that I was deceiving her, ANGRY that I had to shell out even more in legal fees and WEIRDLY HAPPY as she is suing me because she (and her new lawyer) cannot properly read a financial statement. Fun Fact: assuming I had $45,000 stashed away, she asked me if I owned a Villa. I love that word; it sounds so international! It's also preposterous, a Gay Villa in Palm Springs or Wilton Manors would certainly be at least $500,000!

We have our day in court and the judge asks the four of us (divorced couple plus our lawyers) to go into a room and resolve our case. Remarkably, my lawyer did just that. On the original divorce documents, we included a date that we would sell the house. He said we should extend the date by one year and now she could live in the home for another year and live for free. Why was it free? Because we were short selling our home and had stopped paying the mortgage. So – long story short – we changed one number on the original divorce documents. That was the entire stupid second lawsuit.

It speaks to so many consistent themes of our relationship – 'magical' thinking, unnecessary spending (over $3,000 in legal expenses), wasted time and energy. Being divorced and being free was about not only moving forward emotionally but also living a simpler life with a significant reduction in drama.

B	I	N	G	O
You've ruined my life	You're naïve if you think the alimony is enough	All your friends just tell you what you want to hear	Don't come out to the children – they're not ready/you'll lose them forever	You're focused on sex and your new life, the children are my focus
I'm asking for money, but it's for the children	You don't know how to communicate to our children	It's Because You're GAY!!!	We don't need to talk to a child psychologist for other professional	If you hadn't left, EVERYTHING would be okay – our life would be better
I know what's best for our children	You're deluded/ checked out as a parent	I will always choose the kids, even to my own detriment	The kids know you have money and are refusing to use it	God will always provide for me, no matter what you do/don't do

From an emotional perspective, the divorce and second court case didn't settle anything between us. She had been in control for most of our relationship and she had no intention of letting that go. There's a darker side to this fight, one that has repeated itself many times over. My coming out was a blow to her world – she was losing her primary source of income, her housecleaner and her babysitter when she wanted to get away. More importantly, she viewed our soon-to-be-ending relationship as a waste. I 'stole' twenty years of her life, her good years when she was thin and had great skin. The divorce was all about payback for what I did to her and the children, that I owed her. Whenever anything even remotely 'gay' came up in conversation, it was immediately shot down. I was not permitted to expose "her" children to any of that. We have completely different world views – she sees her life purpose as protecting the children from my circle of friends, assuming that we are all deviants.

For years after the divorce, we continued our toxic family dynamic:

HER	HER VIEW OF ME
My decisions on what is needed or best for the children are sacrosanct, you will abide by them	You gave up any parental rights when you left our home, you have irrevocably tarnished our children
I will not involve you in any financial decisions for the children	Figure out how to pay for whatever I decide
You are not involved or included in my weekends with the children	I need to approve any and all activities during your weekend; I reserve the right to contact you anytime over the weekend and it's okay for the children to text me to express their dissatisfaction or if they're not getting their way
My weekends with the children are private	I expect my children to give me a full report of their weekend with you and I will call you on Sunday night to tell you what you've done wrong

My weekends with the kids were invariably the same – after returning the children to her, she would call about an hour later to scold me for some major issue that damaged our children. I was always shocked by the call – there would be zero drama or unresolved issues while we were together, but somehow there was always something after the fact, adding to the many ways that I was a disappointment. Finally, I called out the bullshit – why did these problems only come up AFTER they left me? Were the children directed to not discuss anything with me or was she fabricating drama and her ability to solve it as a way to exalt herself? I'll never know the truth but it led to where we are now – I have trouble believing in what she and the children tell me. I seem to receive select information, on a need-to-know basis. I cannot be trusted with the whole story.

The "Gay Dad Divorce Bingo" was an attempt to document the insanity – I think I created it about a year after the divorce. Finding patterns and realizing that the same excuses were repeated allowed me to see that for her, there was only one family story, and she's the hero and I'm the villain. Ironically, the Bingo card helped my friend Larry, another late bloomer gay dad – he realized that his ex-wife was acting similarly. He laminated a Bingo card and scanned it while on the phone with her and turned it into a game as she fills up the squares!

I can see how I'm painting a one-sided story here and I'll repeat this many times, I am not blameless nor do I pretend to be a saint. I'm trying to capture the lunacy - a false narrative that afforded my ex-wife all of the praise and admiration for our children's successes while assigning all of their problems or disappointments to me. She can't seem to figure out that she has created her own difficult life – a working mother raising two children by herself, she has no support system as far as I know. She spends little time or money on herself – everything is for the children. She has raised 'perfect, polite children' that are not problematic and are exceptional students. Some believe that 'it takes a village to raise a child, ' but she bucks that trend– she controls everything. She would rather reach out to a stranger for support or advice before allowing me to be intimately involved with any decisions for our children.

Here's a story that highlights control, with some skewed thinking thrown in. My son's social interactions were limited growing up – he never slept away from home by himself until he was sixteen. The first time was a sleepover church camp in Panama City Beach. Ironically, I had visited that part of Florida a couple of times, I have a friend with a gorgeous home on Front Beach Road. My son was nervous and I suggested my friend could assist if necessary. When I shared that I knew someone in the area that could help in the case of an emergency, his reply was "of course you do." My son did not want an outsider involved – by definition, a friend of mine was not trustworthy. One week before the trip my son declares that he doesn't feel like going. My ex-wife decides to solve the problem in her special way: she secretly books a room at the same hotel and doesn't tell the camp and my son visited her daily. I'm hoping that you're seeing this as kooky and somewhat creepy. That's the weird decision-making that I struggle to understand – when is she going to let go? How can she not see how wrong this is?

Another example of the 'almost normal' thinking occurred a few years later when she met another divorced teacher. This other woman had two older sons and had recently split up with her husband after he came out of the closet. Yes, this woman was living the same life as her and my ex-wife thought it would be a great idea if the boys met. My son could learn from someone with similar experiences.

> *QUICK NOTE – I think this is a wonderful idea, I appreciate that she wanted to support and educate our children. But wait, let's talk about that execution…*

My son meets with this college-aged young man twice – movies and bowling. From my limited knowledge both went well. However, she secretly paid the other guy $50.00 each time, it's like she rented him for a playdate. As with the Panama City Beach hotel room, I just don't understand the logic.

Chapter Seven

December 2019 – Control, Control, and Even More Control

In addition to her children, students and co-workers, my ex-wife's social network includes her church – she and the children belong to a megachurch (congregation is over 38,000 across eight locations). Years earlier we joined a Baptist church and even attended a bible study class (we were desperate to fit in and make friends). Friendly reminder, we were both raised Catholic and both children were baptized in the Catholic church. But if you want to be associated with the right kind of people in North Georgia, you better attend services on Sunday, and don't go practicing the wrong religion! We weren't looking for salvation and did not have a personal relationship with Jesus. We were attempting to look like other young couples with children: dress up and attend a Baptist church, with our children playing non-competitive sports (my son: soccer and basketball, my daughter: soccer and cheerleading) and enjoying Vacation Bible School in the summer. If we had to abandon our religious upbringing to ensure that we weren't social pariahs, then no worries!

All kidding aside, this megachurch that they now attend supports the community and preaches the golden rule about being a better person. However, on more than one occasion, my ex-wife suggested that I 'make things right with Jesus.' I can understand her need to find a community but I can't reconcile what is her ultimate goal – has God forgiven her for her past? Of course not – she doesn't need it; she has always only thought of her children and their needs. More importantly, her advice is for me to absolve myself so that I can avoid burning in Hell. As you have probably guessed, it's not Jesus that I should ask for forgiveness, it's her.

Even though we lived about 20 miles apart physically, it felt like we were in different times – I represent the present and she embodies some mythic 'better times' from the past. Simply put, I lived in the dangerous city and she's in the safe suburbs. There's a lot to unpack with how our views are so divergent – she sees others that are not like her as threats and I just see people. Where I lived, there were mixed-race, old, young, and LGBTQ+ families – it's diverse. I didn't live in the Gayborhood (yes that's the name of a real app you can download and yes that app is on my phone). Where she lives is homogenous – it's different politically, it's mostly one religion and almost all Caucasian. All of her shopping needs can be met locally or online so there's no reason to risk going into the city. Her world has become significantly smaller – I would argue that she has stopped growing. She lives in a bubble – I can only assume that her life is a constant feedback loop of people that look and believe and act the same and the others that think differently are a threat, they cannot be trusted.

I bet you're thinking that she is on social media constantly, commiserating with people that are just like her, fighting the good fight to protect traditional values and feeling persecuted 24/7, traditional victimization. Here's a twist – you're wrong. She views social media as the decline in social discourse and wishes that we retained old-school methods of communication. I'm not talking about the 1950's or Emily Post, her ideal is Victorian-era letter correspondence. Yep, can't make this shit up.

My coming out opened my eyes to my previously narrow existence – and that was before my ex-wife lived the cocooning existence that binds her and our children. When we were married we lived by so many rules and illogical thinking – it's like I escaped from a cult. Even though coming out was mostly about finding myself and finally realizing what a healthy & happy existence looks like, I also knew that the old life we were living was seriously fucked up and I didn't want to pass that on to my children. I miss seeing my kids every day, I wish I was an active part of their lives. They'll never know that my world is full of loving and supportive friends, neighbors, and co-workers; I want to share that with them. I'm truly happy and that's the role model that I'd love to be for them. They are still beholden to their mother (my son is 22, his sister is 19) and they don't want to know me. My daughter said it plainly, "dad, that's your life, not our life."

From my ex-wife's perspective, my current life and my friendships are a fallacy - I have created this false illusion that I am a wonderful and supportive father who's misunderstood by his children, but I'm really a selfish, sociopathic monster. When I came out of the closet, it wasn't courageous or brave or anything that should be celebrated. I was a liar and had ruined our children's lives permanently. I need to suffer; I don't deserve to be happy. I am a bad person and there was no way that I should be rewarded for my big reveal. I am a fraud and she alone continues to know the 'real me.' How does she show her contempt for me? In a word, judgment. She feels that it is her responsibility to judge me. The divorce was eight years ago and she's still doing it. Unfortunately for me, it's now a learned behavior for my children. I will share stories and details later, but the quick summary is that as my children have gotten older, they have grown LESS accepting of my life and my community. You would think that the opposite would happen – as young people mature; they see the world they have a greater understanding that all of us have baggage and that not every relationship is perfect (as I learned about my parents). And it's not the being gay part – her brother is gay and the children have known that forever. My sin is unforgivable. That's where we are now - I am free from my tormentor, I am financially secure and have a loving and supportive husband and network of friends. But to achieve my happiness, it cost me plenty – I lost my children.

I gave her all the power when we were together and despite my personal growth, I'm embarrassed to say that she still has a certain hold over me. Why do I still let this happen? It's the kids. There's a part of me that doesn't fight back to keep the peace and hope that somehow, someday my children will come back to me, or they will at least come to an understanding of why I made certain decisions. It sucks when you hear about divorced families that get along, plus there are stories of dads that come out of the closet and they resolve their issues with their ex-wives and live happily ever after, separately. It's ironic that I lived in a great home with a pool in the backyard and a super one-bedroom apartment in the basement. It's not crazy to imagine a scenario where we all lived together and become a blended family.

The thing that I hate, what tears me up inside, is how my children see me. They keep secrets from me, they reveal almost nothing about themselves and the absolute worst is when my daughter sends me a text or e-mail that clearly has been written by her mother (see example below). I can't tell if they think that they're clever and fooling me or if they just don't care if I know. All their actions and emotions are some form of deception, withholding information is a form of control. When we were married, separated, and first divorced, I complained to my ex-wife that the children did not respect me as an adult, they treated their father worse than their mother or any teacher. There were instances when I saw my children interact with other adults and I was so proud of how they represented themselves (and by proxy, me); they were well-behaved, polite, charming and funny. The fact that they treat absolute strangers better than their father has always been a slap in the face. It's like they have a constant rage against me that can never be constrained. It reminds me of Pitbulls – loving, gentle creatures that are great dogs and wonderful around children, but if they are raised to hurt and hate and never feel true love, they are forever dangerous. I love my children but I must admit that I don't know them anymore, I am a (presumably unsafe) stranger to them.

> Buying a car:
>
> 1. I truly thought that you were going to give my brother and I your old black Sorento when you bought a new car. Most parents pass down their cars, like your dad did. I was really sad and shocked that you didn't give it to me on my 16th birthday.
>
> 2. I'm a straight-A student and I always give 100% effort in my studies. I'm 100% trust-worthy and a good driver. I'm getting my drivers license in January and need you to go out with me and get a safe, low-mile car. I also babysit and earn gas money.
>
> 3. Buying a safe car for your kids is a rite of passage and parents usually look forward to the prospect of car shopping with their child. I want to be able to be safe and drive like all the other kids at school.
>
> 4. My brother and I have been one of the few kids to not have cars in high school. It's embarrassing and prevents us from accessing internships and having normal, independent social lives.
>
> Thank you.

This e-mail was "written" by my daughter in December 2019 - she is disappointed that I didn't give her my previous car that was recalled by the dealer. This is just how a sixteen-year-old communicates, isn't it? What's hilarious is that at the time of this e-mail, she didn't have her license! Earlier that year my ex-wife informed me that the public high school (enrollment: 2,988) told her that her children were among a handful of students on campus that <u>didn't</u> have a car. Sounds legit, right?

My husband always wanted children and when we first dated, one of the things he found attractive in me was that I was an active father. It's a shame that it's devolved this way - I wish they would meet the great guy that has captured my heart. He's a good man by himself and he makes me an even better man, we have a healthy and loving relationship. I want them to see that we respect and trust each other, we laugh and communicate in ways that enhance the love we share. We don't play games to achieve what we want. We're together because each of us makes the other happy - it's that simple.

To the best of my knowledge, my ex-wife has not been in a relationship since our divorce, much less a single date – in her words, I ruined men for her. For my children it's a double whammy – they revere their mother, a woman who has given up on having any type of romantic relationship and they have nothing but contempt for their father, a man who is in a loving, committed marriage.

Chapter Eight

January 2018 – The Curious Adventures of Trivia Man & Quiz Bowl Boy

Starting in second grade, my son finally attended public school. He received special needs services (occupational therapy) but for the most part, he could more-or-less blend into a classroom with typical students. He was tremendously smart, but it was the other parts of his personality that were out of the ordinary. From an intelligence perspective, he was in the 99th percentile across all standardized tests, however many parts of him were years behind – it's like he was trapped inside his body for 3-4 years and wasn't able to experience developmental milestones. As a result, he was immature in a variety of ways, he would experience emotional outbursts if frustrated, sad or angry. He knew he was ahead of the classroom but he lacked any emotional intelligence, could not read social cues, had difficulty sharing, and had no patience. You get the idea – he was a big ol' Sheldon Cooper from the television series *The Big Bang Theory*. That character knew he possessed superior mental acuity and became frustrated when others couldn't catch up.

Every calendar year brought my son closer to everyone else's orbit – you could almost say that he was a 'learning computer.' He went from WEIRD in elementary school from GIFTED BUT DIFFERENT in middle school to WICKED SMART AMONG HIS PEERS in high school. Along the way we accomplished something that we weren't exactly sure would ever happen – when he transitioned from elementary school to middle school, we ripped up his individual education plan (IEP), the school form that designates some type of special needs, you need it to receive special services. He was slowly improving and by the time that middle school came around, he looked and acted neuro-typical.

Canceling his IEP was powerful for us. We did it, we gave our son a fighting chance to learn, laugh and love as an adult. He was not yet a teenager and we didn't know where he was heading, but at least we had HOPE for his future. Removing our son 'out of the school system' fed a couple of our family's peculiarities – his diagnosis was a secret and we wanted to bury that secret. We didn't want him to be outed by a teacher or administration, that somehow his condition was shameful. Moving to a new school was escaping our past, restarting and creating a new identity. If it sounds like I'm telegraphing that our son's condition was a parable for my homosexuality that was still in the closet, it's because I am.

He received occupational therapy because his fine and gross motor control were behind his peers – he struggled with tying his shoes, using a knife to cut food, or throwing a ball. I felt bad for him because it must have been so difficult to fit in with other kids. Learning a new sport came naturally to the triplets and before my son was born and when he was a baby, I dreamt of him becoming an athlete – that he would become tall like my ex-wife's family and possess some coordination and athletic ability from my side, and he would have a supportive dad who would take an interest in his sport(s), help him practice, take him to games. I wanted to create the idyllic father: son relationship that I never received – you could argue that I wanted to heal myself through him. My son did play basketball and soccer in some recreational leagues, but we didn't make him stick with it. We wanted to expose him to boys and girls outside of his school, to learn how to win and lose, typical "learn how to play fair and have fun" bullshit that we attempt to teach our kids but don't really believe or even practice in real life.

Without even trying, my son found his niche, where he belonged. The magical world of Academic Bowls! Looking back, it's obvious that he had all the right tools to be a quiz bowl ninja: raw intellectual power combined with quick thinking and competitive spirit (PS – I'm taking credit for that last part). We lived in an area where Academic Bowls (it's like Teen Jeopardy) began in Middle School, some as early as Elementary School. Of course the team wanted him – he was smart and fast! When he joined he was not named captain, something that frustrated and confused him because he was the smartest player on the team. During one competition, the captain chose another player for the final question. As the question was asked, my son was visibly upset that he was not chosen, he knew the answer and was anxious as that question decided the match. Unfortunately, the other player got the question wrong and my son screamed at the captain, then started crying. He wasn't ready to lead just yet, still unable to fully control his emotions. The next year he was the captain and made those types of executive decisions – I am beaming with pride as I remember this and recall his emotional maturity. He was a growing young man and fit perfectly within his tribe.

I thoroughly enjoyed going to all of his events – they're normally played at a high school for the entire Saturday. It was strange – the children were accompanied by their teacher/coach and me - no other parent regularly attended. I would sit in the back at each match and watch my son work his magic with the buzzer. Not unlike watching my sister glide past the competition in track, it was emotionally satisfying to see my son win, and sometimes crush, over the competition. Remember that these are all incredibly smart kids! It was amazing to see that he was the best of the best – usually one of the top 2-3 players in every tournament. If he played, they were competitive.

I'm pretty ecstatic that my son turned out just like me – competitive, but in a different way. He hated losing even more than he loved winning and I was right there with him, my emotions teetered up and down with the team's fortunes. It was intense – my heart would be pounding in my chest as a close match went down to the wire. I was living vicariously through him and his impressive talents – I couldn't answer more than 5-10% of the questions that were asked and certainly not at the speed that he processed them.

The last tournament of his that I attended did not end well. His academic advisor knew that I was single and offered to set me up with another teacher…a female one. I responded, "actually I date guys." A few hours later, I shared this conversation with my son and he flipped out – immediately he said, "no one cares that you're a fag!" He then responded that he would be bullied in school if others found out that he had a gay father. I was so hurt by this – my children were embarrassed by me; they were fine that I was gay as long as it didn't affect them personally or impacted their lives. It hurt even more because it was my son, I had a natural affinity for him and I was convinced that he would come around and be one of my supporters. After that outburst I was no longer invited to any tournaments – it was the beginning of how I became invisible to my children.

My love of trivia and collecting (and remembering!) random, useless information started at an early age and among my friends and co-workers, people would reach out to me to help them remember a song or movie quote. Like my son, I am just wired that way. Even today, I love to research a topic and immerse myself in random facts – you never know when someone will ask you "who sang the one-hit wonder 96 Tears?" and you'll be prepared with the answer, "? and the Mysterians."

When I started my coming out journey (still married, still in the closet), I met my first gay bear friend and the first guy I ever kissed, my buddy Jacob. He called himself an Educated Hick and man, he fit the bill – his breadth of knowledge was impressive! Before we met, Jacob had a partner named Steve and they were together for three years before Steve died from a sudden heart attack. Jacob became withdrawn after that and never left his house except for work and grocery shopping. Every night he would stay home and watch Jeopardy while plowing through packs of Wal-Mart brand cigarettes. We met for coffee in a Burger King parking lot and there was an instant connection, a kinship. You know my side – I wanted just one friend and was figuring out who I was. Jacob was lonely too – I didn't realize that our dinners/trivia matches were the beginning of him coming out of his shell; he finally decided to live in the outside world and not sit home and watch television and fall asleep in his recliner. It's so heartwarming that I was helping him as he was doing the same for me.

When we played bar trivia, we were formidable from the start: and he knew History, Geography, Science and Religion. My specialties were Sports, Music, Movies and Pop Culture. We were an awesome combination! Beginning in Spring 2013, we tried to have dinner once a week and play together. I lied to my wife and told her that he was a co-worker, that this was a work team – that was the only way I was allowed to leave the house on a school night. I'm not proud of that minor deception, but playing trivia brought me so much joy – I was good at it and I was doing something for myself. It sounds so childish that I couldn't tell her the truth, but it was the only way that I could escape from her ever-watchful eyes.

Even though we were just trivia buddies, I soon developed feelings for Jacob – I thought he was 'the one.' At the time I told my friend Jason, "he's damaged like me, we're perfect for each other." I must have sounded like a pre-teen falling hard for their first crush. Even though I was in my 40s, I was now allowing myself to recognize my sexual attraction to other men and articulating it. It was my "gay puberty."

Before everything went south between my son and me, he often joined us for trivia and a free meal. Of course I wanted him to be on our team (dramatically increasing our chances of winning each week, tee hee), but the underlying benefit was that we sat around and watched sports and played trivia and talked about stupid stuff. It was so boring and so…normal. Yes, this is what other families did with their teenage children, this is what living looked like.

Jacob & Peter – a powerful combination

Losing my son hurts the most. Not only was I super proud of his triumphs but I also loved his dry humor-sarcasm-snark. I also thought he was on "my team," if you know what I mean. I don't know his sexual orientation or his interest in girls or boys and I don't care – I just want him to be happy. I imagine this scenario, I replay it often in my head – my college-age son meets people from around the country, they get to know each other and they tell their stories. He talks about his parent's divorce – what does he say? How does he frame it?

> *I was born in Florida, lived in Chicago for a couple of years, but spent the majority of my childhood in Atlanta with my younger sister. Our family was normal until 2013 when my parents split up. My father decided that he was gay and left my mom and us. We saw him every other weekend but I didn't like going to his apartment – it wasn't a real home; it wasn't our home. My mom worked hard to maintain a happy home for us while my dad abandoned us and paraded around Atlanta and the rest of the country with his PRIDE flag. He was always pushing his "gayness" on us – forcing us to meet his friends. It made me uncomfortable and it was painfully obvious that he was just showing us off. He went to my academic bowl tournaments but he ruined that by announcing to my coach that he was a big homo – why does he have to make it about him? What's wrong with him? I was finally done with him when I became a senior – I got a tuition scholarship from his company and he decided that he wasn't going to help pay for college – my mom has to pay for everything. He makes lots of money and spends it on himself and his bear friends. He abandoned his family. My mom is the only one I can rely on.*

Of course I'm hoping for his epiphany – a breakthrough. The point where he questions this one-sided viewpoint and wonders if there's more to the story. I also imagine that he's hearing from classmates that have more severe backgrounds; they've had more struggles and/or shittier parents. Will he ever wonder, "well, maybe I didn't have it so bad?" He loves his mother and would never want to hurt her – would he see it as a betrayal if he ever reaches out to me?

I do recognize that this may sound like whining – I am venting, processing my emotions and grieving. I want my son to be in my life, I want to help him grow into an awesome man and I want my experiences and network of friends and business associates to help him find his way in life and help navigate his career progression. I want what every father wants. And it's still weird that he doesn't want that from me – I guess I am still toxic, I have no value.

I must admit that the "doesn't support me in college" line is curious and annoying. His tuition is covered via a state award and he receives scholarships from my work and my industry trade association (combined $6,000 annually). And my ex-wife received child support for him while he is in school and you would expect that she used those monies toward college. I assume that she didn't and painted me as the bad guy for any student loans he may need.

What are his educational expenses? How much has my ex-wife contributed? I don't know the answer to either – more examples of selective information sharing. I cannot count the number of times that I have been presented a receipt for something that she has already purchased, asking me to contribute or reimburse her. I don't know if it's passive-aggressive but it's certainly another form of control. Only she knows what's best for the children, she doesn't want any involvement or discussion on what is needed/what is purchased. And I am expected to provide funding, even if it's after the fact. Admittedly, that way did work when we first separated. Finally, I put my foot down and simply stated that if there's an expense that I was not consulted on or even made aware of beforehand, then I'm not paying for it.

Divorce 101 states that you should unconditionally love your children, never blame the divorce on them, never speak ill of your ex-spouse and never, ever talk about money. A simple conversation with my daughter revealed what was going on with my ex-wife and my son's child support. We were talking about my son in college and I shared with her that generally, child support ends when each kid becomes 18 years old. In Georgia, if the children are close enough in age, child support ends when the <u>youngest</u> child turns eighteen. I said, "I'm supporting your brother, even though he doesn't live with your mother." Her response was, "but we need that money to cover our everyday expenses." Her answer made me laugh and cry. The memories came flooding back – the month-to-month struggles, not living within our means, no planning for the future. That's still going on, just without me.

I want to save my daughter from that type of existence, that 'subsistence'. But I haven't figured out how to help her without sacrificing my hard-earned liberty. Am I wrong for wanting to stay liberated? Does she even want my help? Or just my money? Was this type of learned behavior happening while I was still married to her mother? Was my silent acquiescence teaching her that living beyond your means was acceptable? These types of questions haunt me. But I'm going to keep going forward and keep doing the best I can. Partially because I know Joy is reading this and she will go all "mama bear" on me if I allow myself to regress. She is my favorite PITA sometimes.

Chapter Nine

June 2015 – Clothes Maketh the Man – Mr. Speedo Man

In starting my dating life, I transformed via a "Queer Eye for the Straight Guy / Midlife Crisis Makeover'" mash-up. I was newly out of the closet (i.e., a Baby Gay) and was updating my wardrobe with brighter and tighter clothes. That last part was another revelation, an example of how I didn't know myself, didn't allow myself to shine. My boring-ass wardrobe had remained unchanged for years. However, in a few short weeks I discovered that all my measurements were wrong. I felt like my old attire was a set of shackles and my new look was happier, it was just me. I've heard that women feel amazing when they find a great bra that fits. Before I was so uncomfortable in my body, my clothes did nothing to show it off. Now my clothes are ENHANCING my body! Here's what I mean:

- BEFORE – 34" x 30" pants, large shirts, large boxers for underwear
- AFTER – 32" x 32" pants, medium shirts, medium boxer briefs for underwear

It was incredible that I was physically the same person, but now I was allowing my wardrobe to be part of my identity, which required multiple sessions with retail therapists. Seriously, I needed to update my look and while I did have some discretionary money every month (remember, I divorced my money problems), I didn't want to overspend. Combining that with my love for a bargain, I became a HUGE Goodwill shopper. To this day, almost fifty percent of my wardrobe is from thrifting expeditions.

Getting a great price for something of value began when I was young – my mother loved garage sales. When I was old enough to drive, I followed in her footsteps, getting up at the crack of dawn every Saturday to hunt for bargains. As a quick side note, I obviously wasn't partying on Friday nights, which allowed for early weekend morning adventures. My youth was NOT wild and crazy!

As much as I may not want to admit it, getting something for less than what others have paid, from discount or negotiation, is a New England thing. It's not about saving money per se, it's that we're smarter than everyone else and we bucked the system. It's the opposite of an inferiority complex– it's a superiority complex! I'm laughing at myself as I type this – many people from the Northeast believe that they're better than other parts of the country and they don't care if you know, don't care if you think they're snobby. It's the truth and sometimes the truth hurts.

I bought lots of clothes – thrifting became AT LEAST a twice-week adventure and I quickly learned which Goodwill's had the right kind of clientele that would build my size medium fashion empire. I'm fortunate that a good portion of the dozens (probably hundreds) of dress shirts that I purchased still have the dry cleaning tags on them – SCORE! And when you purchase so many items for $6.36 at a time, it's hard to justify paying full retail prices. That buying spree lasted about two years. It was a magical time, combining the joy of discovery with the freedom to wear something bold or flashy. I wasn't worried about wearing a shirt or outfit that was too gay. I was gay!

It was exhilarating to blossom into a fashionista at my work, especially when I traveled and/or met with customers. I'm a marketing guy, so I had that freedom to wear bolder ties, to NOT wear a blue blazer, to add a pop of color via a pocket square – maybe all three at the same time! I managed our largest industry trade show and our VP of Sales wanted us to be professional but casual. Suit jackets, a collared shirt and NO TIES were the required attire for all men. But Peter is no ordinary man! I was on the show floor most of the time and I wanted to make an impact, to stand out among my peers. My "required attire" was to always wear a tie (often a bow tie, one that I tied myself) and a pocket square, it was my personal branding statement. The first time that I wore a bow tie to the formal dinner at our national sales meeting, I couldn't believe how many (presumably straight) guys came up to me and complimented my look. They were impressed that I had the guts to look different than everyone else.

Being different, being me was what this was all about! I was so surprised at this revelation – previously I used clothes to hide who I was – it wasn't about color or fashion or flash. It was just a thing. Flipping the script, now clothes were a personality statement – I was bold, exciting, and simply put, I was happy and fun.

I won't share too many details, I also learned quickly that I could rock a tiny bathing suit – my preference is a Brazilian-style square cut. I don't know how to explain it any other way – I have this body and I see it every day. It's nothing special to me, I wasn't particularly attracted to it (remember, I like big bears). But when I put on this thin layer of fabric, somehow my body looked attractive. It showed off my muscular legs, which I see as my greatest physical asset. I felt sexy! My burgeoning confidence inside of me allowed me to feel comfortable prancing around in a tight suit, leaving nothing to the imagination in the front or the back.

My bathing suit collection came in handy during the summer pool party season. Weekend-long bear pool parties called 'Bear Runs' are a year-round affair with kitschy names like Tidal Wave, Bear Hunt, Drenched Fur, Beef Dip, Lazy Bear and Midwest Bearfest. This list doesn't include Bear Weekend in Provincetown, that's an entire week of thousands of gay bears that take over the town. Logistically, the event books an entire medium-sized hotel for the weekend – they almost always sell out. There's a practical reason – men attend these so that they can be gay adults – drinking and wearing tiny bathing suits and flashy outfits. You don't want to expose (pun intended) straight people to this, especially children. Events like these are not easily understood by those outside of the community, so it's best to not shock them, to not subject them to it.

The more subtle reason why you don't want outsiders to attend these events is that the men want to be amongst their community, with the freedom to be around others like them, to express themselves and not be judged. Trust me, there are still plenty of drama queens and guys that feel that it's their responsibility to be bitchy, but the point is that we're all together – we're in a safe bubble. I've always been slender and I can't fully appreciate the constant struggles that big men face. Everything in our culture is about being skinny and for all my bear friends, being big is seen through a negative light in almost every way possible – they are that size because they're eating too much or not exercising enough or just plain lazy. Clothes are another disaster for bigger guys – many of the traditional stores don't offer sizes above XL and the fashionable ones that cater to larger men are fantastically expensive.

Bear Runs mean tiny bathing suits, so the entire pool is filled with large hairy men with little covering their bodies. This is another emotional benefit for bigger guys to attend events like these – there's no need to cover up or hide your body. Plus, the audience WANTS you to wear as little as possible – they're attracted to it! When gay men get together and there's alcohol involved, there will invariably be some type of kissing too - it happens every weekend at every gay bar in the United States. Because gay men cannot be expressive in most areas of the country (no hand holding, certainly no kissing), it's quite liberating to just be yourself, to not have to check if anyone straight is watching. We're just guys who are hanging out with friends and having some adult beverages. Many people wouldn't think twice when it happens in your local watering hole. It's the same here, just a change in audience and wardrobe. Since I came out of the closet, Atlanta Bear Fest provided me a 'gay baptism' (PS – that's not a thing, I just made up that term). For bears that live in small towns or nowhere near a major city or if they're still in the closet, these events are an opportunity to reconnect and recharge with your community, to not feel alone.

I thoroughly enjoyed all the Bear Runs that I attended. First, math was on my side! There's usually about one skinny guy to nine or ten bears, so the odds are always in my favor. Skinny guys are called Chasers, aka we chase after bears. Remember that this is a BEAR event, so most of the audience consists of bears who are attracted to bears. These events have an annual theme and there's always some type of costumed affair and an LGBTQ+ friendly comedian. As a textbook extrovert who's now comfortable with his sexual identity and receives positive feedback when he wears skimpy outfits, you know I went all in on having fun, camping it up, really soaking in the atmosphere.

One time I attended a 'Loving Your Bear Body' workshop. Of the 24 attendees, 22 were men. The other two were Trans – they had facial and body hair, but they did not yet have male sexual organs. Along the same lines as the overall Bear Run, this was a spiritual event that used mediation and various exercises to explore and get in touch with your body, learning to embrace your shape and receive positive reinforcement from the attendees. And we're also naked. It's not sexual or anything like that, think of it like a nudist colony. I've told you before that I like my body so why would I attend something like this? I believe this answer can be best explained by our last exercise: you get in groups of three and each of you has the floor for two minutes. The concept is to ask for something you've always wanted, to command it from the other two. When this was announced, I knew exactly what I wanted – I visualized it immediately. While sitting on the floor, I asked one guy to be in front of me, close enough that our faces were inches apart and his arms could hug me. Essentially we were straddling each other. I asked the second one to sit behind me, his belly to my back, with his arms around me. For two minutes I asked them to squeeze me intently and to tell me that I was a good person. I immediately started crying and they went to work consoling me, telling me that I was not only a good guy, but I was good enough for whatever empty part of myself that needed to hear that and be reassured.

I guess that hole in my heart left by my father is still in need of some repair.

Chapter Ten

February 2017 - Boston Sports Fans – from Lovable Losers to Obnoxious Sore Winners

I cannot say enough how much I adore and miss Massachusetts. I love the seasons and I sort of miss my wicked accent, although no snow shoveling in California is great! The triplets were an energetic bunch and to help keep us busy and out of my mom's hair, we were constantly enrolled in organized sports; fall soccer, spring baseball and the Knights of Columbus swim team in the summer. My brother and I were average athletes when we were young, although I did play varsity soccer, basketball, and tennis in high school. Maybe that sounds impressive? It's not, my high school was super small – if you tried out, you made the team.

Although our sister was the same age (three minutes older than me, one minute younger than my brother), she was the best athlete among us, the best in our family, maybe even in our town. It started with swimming – she was fantastic at the breaststroke; my strength was the backstroke and my brother took care of freestyle. If you know anything about competitive swimming, you will recognize that the Leahy triplets were three-fourths of a mixed Individual Medley team. My brother and I were competent swimmers – sometimes we'd win gold, but most of the time we did not. My sister was consistent – she hardly ever lost, she was all legs and she carried us on more than one occasion. In high school she was even more impressive. Our oldest sister was the captain of the girl's track team and my triplet sister followed in her footsteps. She performed well in regional competitions and even ran track in college at Northeastern University.

I attended a few of her meets and she was stunning as I watched her run around the track. She was a natural and as her long legs churned she made the other girls look like they were traveling at 75% of their fastest speed. I was never jealous of her abundance of God-given talents, but I do wonder what would have happened if she was pushed to become an elite-level athlete. Again, she competed at the collegiate level, but there is a part of me that wonders how exceptional she could have been.

I've mentioned that my father was not affectionate and not active in his children's lives. My sister's track prowess was the exception to the rule. He was especially proud when she won the local Turkey Trot and came home with a free turkey and in one especially memorable event, he reprinted the local sports page into a 2' x 3' poster board that showcased one of her many successful track meets. In this contest, the other team was not very strong so my sister's coach let her participate in every event, track AND field. Amazingly, she won like 7-8 medals that day, including the discus and the shot put, which I knew she didn't know how to throw. My dad wasn't good with praise and was unfortunately absent for a significant portion of my childhood, but this was his way to say, at least to my sister, that he loved her and was proud of her.

Watching and playing sports has always been a critical part of my identity and I will never change from being a passionate (read: obnoxious) Boston sports fan. How much are Boston sports integral to my upbringing? How about the fact that the first words I ever said were 'Bobby Orr?' As God as my witness it's the truth. By the time I was three-and-a-half, my mother realized that my triplet brother and sister were talking and saying full sentences but I was not. Yes, I realize this looks exactly like my son's history, but they are completely different situations. I could say simple words (milk, cookie, ball), but nothing else was coming out. My mother took me to our pediatrician and he tried to reassure her – he said "well, you know that Albert Einstein didn't learn to speak until he was five." My mother responded honestly, "I don't want my son to be Einstein." Soon after, my father came home with the iconic Bobby Orr "horizontal cheering" poster and while we looked at it, I said "BAH-BEE OR-RRR."

My father played hockey in high school and as an adult, he enjoyed watching the Boston Bruins on television; sometimes my brother and I would watch with him. He didn't like basketball or football and while he did love the 'cursed' Red Sox, he gave up on major league baseball after the 1994 strike. He called them 'bums' and he was done with them. When I moved away from Boston later that year, the Red Sox were still lovable losers, the Patriots were years away from their twenty-year dynasty. Little did I know that both of those franchises would become sports championship juggernauts in the 2000s and that the Celtics and Bruins would also win during the same decade.

IMHO, the event that transformed the trajectory of all Boston sports was the 2001 Super Bowl victory of the New England Patriots. I'll provide my armchair therapist assessment in a minute, but I want to set the stage for what happened that night and how yours truly 'might' have helped the Pats win. At that time the four Boston sports franchises had been experiencing a MAJOR championship drought (Red Sox – 83 years, Bruins – 27 years, Celtics – 15 years, Patriots – zero championships) and the Patriots had been to the Super Bowl twice (1985, 1996) and lost badly both times. The game starts and I have no expectation that they'll win – they were predicted to lose by two touchdowns and their opponent, the St. Louis Rams, "The Greatest Show on Turf," had beaten them earlier in the season. Helmed by a young Tom Brady at quarterback and a previously-unsuccessful Bill Belichick at Head Coach, it was a scrappy team that relied on an aggressive defense and a solid, if not unspectacular, running game.

I'm sure that you know the story – I have most of the big plays stored in my head, especially the last 1:21 of the fourth quarter. The game started beautifully, exactly as the Patriots would have hoped. The Rams were unable to run their traditional offense and the hard-hitting Patriots defense created turnovers and their first score came from the defensive side of the ball (thank you Ty Law!). The Patriots have a large halftime lead and it's not until late in the fourth quarter that the Rams tie the score. Luckily we experienced the first glimpse of Tom Brady magic as he drove down the field at the end of the game with the game-winning field goal as time expired.

I mentioned that I helped and I swear I did…by saying nothing. During halftime I reasoned that if I even made a peep, I would jinx the team. So that's what I did. I sat on my hands and squinted and grimaced as I watched the team's lead fade as time nearly expired. I was resigned to the fact that all my hard work wasn't helping, I could see the writing on the wall. Through our many heartaches, especially with the Red Sox, we had been conditioned to see how this game was going to end – it would be the other team, the other city. Boston was NOT the city of champions at the time. Something had to change to turn around the culture and if you thought the Patriots were going to break that curse, then I would use a quote from my dad and call you 'soft as a sneaker.' The Patriots were not synonymous with winning. They could be very good, but usually they were basement dwellers – never a consistently good team, never a winning mindset. They'd ALWAYS let us down in the past, so why should we expect anything different now? They were NOT a team that you could expect to come through in the clutch. Teams like that don't find ways to win, they usually find new and particularly painful ways to blow it.

But win they did! We didn't realize it at first, but this shocked us in New England - we could win the big game, and we didn't have to define ourselves as losers. The Red Sox World Series victory in 2004 is a larger turning point in Boston sports history – anytime you break 'The Curse of the Bambino' and succeed with the greatest comeback in sports playoff history while beating the hated New York Yankees – that's the once-in-a-lifetime event. I'll cover the Red Sox in the next chapter, but for the moment let's appreciate what Belichick and Brady delivered for the fans. The Patriots were somewhat lucky that day, they were aggressive on defense and the Rams did not adjust, they stuck with their trusted, and incredibly successful, up-tempo offensive plan. The Patriots' mindset that year and for the Brady-Belichick era was about winning, having a smarter game plan than your competitor and clutch performances. The formula worked – over twenty years they went to nine Super Bowls, won six of them and Tom Brady was the MVP for four of them. Tom (we're on a first-name basis, of course we are) had engineered some great comebacks in 2001, including the infamous Tuck Rule playoff game against the Oakland Raiders. All these victories created a new emotion for Pats fans – HOPE. If the team was down at the end of the game, there was always a chance that they could come back – they'd done it before. It's such an amazing and wonderful transformation that it was now important, dare I say a requirement, to watch the whole game. Something could happen! A competitor's lead was never safe! Contrast that with their games from my childhood – if they were behind at halftime, it was likely that they weren't coming back, so it's best to shut off the television now. Even more painful were examples of the team leading in the fourth quarter, and you're watching until the end, and it's then that they finally allow the other team to come back or they make a mistake that allows the other team to score. Those boneheaded plays from a dysfunctional sports franchise were long gone. The Patriots weren't perfect and they didn't win every game, but they were no longer an embarrassment. They gave us a sense of confidence which later blossomed into arrogance.

If you know anything about Tom Brady in the Super Bowl, you'll know that he engineered the greatest comeback in football playoff history when the Patriots beat the Falcons in 2017 – a game where they once trailed 28-3 and were down by nineteen points when the fourth quarter started. That game produced an avalanche of emotions in me. I watched the entire game in a gay bear sports bar in Atlanta, wearing my Tom Brady jersey. The bar was over 99% Falcons fans, there were only three of us that admitted our allegiance to the Pats. During the first half, the Falcons were unstoppable and the Patriots did not look like themselves – even Tom Brady threw a pick-six! I've said it before that we didn't win every game, but we were almost always competitive. That's what sucked about the first half – we weren't playing our best game, we looked slow and we made the opponent look invincible.

Compounding my misery were my 'friends' at the bar – all loving how effortless the game looked for their team and enjoying that Tom Freaking Brady and those damn Patriots were finally going to lose and just maybe, Tom would retire. If you talk to any Boston sports fan and mention the on-air sports personality Max Kellerman, their blood pressure will immediately rise, the hairs on the back of their neck will stand out and their teeth will grit ever so slightly. Max predicted in early 2016 that Tom will 'fall off a cliff' and no longer be an elite quarterback. Amazingly, Tom just won his SEVENTH Super Bowl championship in 2021!

The entire bar seemed to be filled with Max Kellermans – everyone is happy, hooting and hollering. It was a night to remember, finally their long-suffering Falcons (another team that has never won the big game) were going to reach the pinnacle of their sport and they were going to accomplish it by crushing the most hated franchise in the league, my team. My friend Matt came up to me, put his hand on my shoulder and with an inebriated smile said, "it's really good to see you." Our paths had crossed many times – he was the elementary school principal for my children and he hired my ex-wife as a teacher. He was single at the time, semi-ish in the closet and of course I was living in my previous identity.

Now we were face-to-face in a gay bar together with his arm was annoyingly draped on me and I was depressed, stunned and pissed.

Then came the chicken sandwich incident. Yes, if I was going to stay in this damn bar and watch this shitty game with these godforsaken homo Falcons fans, I might as well eat something. Just a simple order – chicken and cheese and bacon. I ordered before halftime and by the time the third quarter started, it still hasn't arrived. Admittedly the bar was packed, but this was a total WTF moment. "Are you fucking kidding me?" I thought to myself. I have to suffer as my team plays its worst game of the season, at the worst possible time, and I can't have a damn chicken sandwich? I swear that the server did it on purpose – I was the enemy that night. When he finally discovers the lost order, we had a decision to make: do we order something to stay in the bar or order something to go or just go home? I don't know why we stayed but we did. It was that sandwich.

For a passionate Patriots fan, the first half of the game was just hell – Tom Brady looked old – OMG was Max Kellerman correct? The second half of the game was incredibly stressful – yes I said stressful and I meant it. I sat on my hands the whole time, nearly passing out from holding my breath. Unlike in early 2002, I think I said a word or two occasionally, but there was no reason to be happy or optimistic. All I wanted was the Patriots to make the score respectable, to not look so shell-shocked. Before their epic comeback, I had given up. As shameful as it is to admit it, it's true. What person in their right mind would predict that the Falcons would play nearly perfect football for nearly three quarters and then the Patriots would turn around and play flawlessly for the last quarter while the Falcons let the game slip away?

As I wasn't a Falcons fan, I wasn't aware of their penchant for blowing leads, for being 'that team' that couldn't come through in the clutch. But the lead was so large and there wasn't enough time! Fox Sports shared a graphic on the screen – when an NFL playoff team had a lead of 19 points or more going into the fourth quarter, they were 93-0. No one had ever blown a lead, no one had ever come back from that deficit. Watching the Patriots in the fourth quarter was like watching my triplet sister run around the track – everything just fell into place. Our little contingent of Patriots fans got happier and maybe just a little bit vocal and the rest of the bar became eerily silent. The Falcons had let them down before, but certainly this time would be different. Matt Ryan, the Falcons quarterback would win the MVP that year with nearly 5,000 yards passing and a 38/7 TD to interception ratio. Certainly Matty Ice was going to come through.

The Patriots tied the game with less than one minute left and before overtime started, there was a coin toss to determine which team would kick and receive. The Patriots choose heads and won that toss. It was then and only then that I knew that the Patriots would win. The overtime period was a fait accompli – Brady methodically drove down the field and led the team to score the winning touchdown. I was beaming on the inside but I knew what I had to do – I had to get out of that bar ASAP. I zipped up my coat, completely covering my jersey and slowly walked to the door. The bar was still full but it felt like a ghost town; everyone's shoulders were collectively slumped forward and they were stunned into silence. There's a scene in the movie <u>The Birds</u> when Tippi Hedren's character is trapped in an attic with dozens of birds. She methodically moves past them, nearly frozen with fear because just one sound or sudden movement would set off the flock and create mayhem. That's what it felt like leaving the bar – I needed to make my move now before the crowd could potentially turn on me.

I was fortunate to experience that sports history while it was happening – how can I ever forget it? For those of us who are Boston sports fans, that game is a wonderful memory, that come-from-behind victory is one for the ages, but it's not the greatest comeback for Beantown. That honor goes to the 2004 Boston Red Sox. Those games, that team, helped heal generations of fans across New England, including my family.

Chapter Eleven

October 2004 – How the 2004 Red Sox Rehabilitated New England and the Leahy's

To best understand why the Red Sox 2004 World Series victory was so emotionally important to New England and my family in particular, some context is appropriate. 2003 was a crappy year for us – once again, the Red Sox suffered another heartbreaking playoff series loss to the Yankees (thankfully the Yanks lost in the World Series, said Mr. Jealous Guy) and earlier that year, my father died at age 77. It was about four months from the time that we found out he was sick until his passing. It started when my father fainted in public – he became dizzy because his high blood pressure medicine was too strong. His medicine was too strong because he had lost a significant amount of weight. Why had he lost so much weight? Because he had stopped eating. And why was he not hungry? Because his unchecked colon cancer had spread to his liver. I shared previously that my father was never sick, despite being thick in the middle. He seldom went to the doctor and specifically, he never scheduled a colonoscopy. Eventually I surmised that my father's side of the family has the colon cancer gene. His brother also suffered from it, my sister had polyps removed when she was pregnant with her daughter and I had some tiny polyps removed when I was in my 40s. I make sure that I get tested regularly – I have many years of happiness to look forward to.

My father's passing wasn't that emotional for me, for obvious reasons. It was the first significant death in my family in quite some time, and it was the first time that our family had to prepare for a wake and funeral. Two things about the wake stick in my mind:

- We arrived at the funeral home and my father was in his casket. His skin had turned quite yellow at the end so the staff did their best to normalize his skin tone. We paid our respects then went out to lunch (seafood of course!) and came back. When I first saw my father, it wasn't strange, but when we came back to the place and he hadn't moved, that's when it hit me.
- When people arrived for the wake, we thanked them for coming – we formed a 'wedding receiving line' of the five children. Of

course we were in birth order (Peter bringing up the rear) and I had to continually develop a creative way to say "thank you for coming" that was slightly different than the rest of my siblings.

Emotions run high when there's a death in the family – my wife's parents drove over 100 miles and paid their respects. It was a wonderful, unexpected gesture and I was touched that they made the trip. My sister had the opposite reaction – she questioned why they were here and what they were doing. Her in-laws also lived across the state and they didn't make the trip, so it was obvious that she was embarrassed and decided to take it out on me. She lashed out at me later in front of everyone when she realized that I didn't cry during the whole affair – she asked if I really loved our father. I mentioned before that my heart had become a stone and it's still that way. I closed the door to our relationship when I was younger. I was sad for my mother and my siblings because they were hurt, but I had lost him so many years ago – there was nothing left of me to feel for him. With time I've come to respect him and admire him from afar, but I'll always see it as a missed opportunity in so many ways: when I became an adult, I did not seek his advice or see him as a friend and when he finally passed, I was engulfed in my stressful, confusing, life-sucking relationship.

My father lived almost 78 years and the Red Sox never won a world series in his lifetime. Their last championship of the twentieth century (1918) was seven years before he was born and he died 18 months before the self-proclaimed 'Gang of Idiots' finally broke through in the 2004 Fall Classic.

For those of you who aren't obsessed with Boston sports like me, I'll spare the play-by-play of this playoff series. The Red Sox and the Yankees were great teams that year and Boston had a great offense. How good? The number nine hitter in the lineup, normally the weakest hitter for any team, won the American League batting title with a .326 average. Quickly the Sox lost the first three games of the series and Game Three was particularly embarrassing, losing 19-8 at home. It was so freaking depressing to see the Yankees hit and hit again, to keep rounding the bases, for more of THEIR numbers to go up on the famous Green Monster manual scoreboard. Somehow the Red Sox eked out a win in Game Four (I will forever love Dave Roberts for THE GREATEST

STOLEN BASE IN RED SOX HISTORY!) and then won the next three games to win the series. No baseball team had ever completed this type of comeback in the 100+ year history of Major League Baseball. And because it was the Yankees, it was as therapeutic as it was exhilarating. I played my part by wearing the same sweatpants/sweatshirt outfit every night during the comeback. I guess you could say that both Peter and the Red Sox were 'ripe' for a victory by Game Seven. Just like my vow of silence during the Patriots' 2001 Super Bowl win, I know in my head that what I'm doing is ridiculous and rather preposterous, but it's a way to feel connected with the team, with the game. Weirdly, it's like you're a contributor or participant, not just an observer.

I treasure so many memories from that series – I mentioned the Game Four ninth-inning steal from Dave Roberts, but that's only part of that one moment. Kevin Millar drew a walk from the normally unflappable Mariano Rivera (who blew the save, OMG!) and Bill Mueller smacked a single to drive in Roberts from second base. I haven't even mentioned other significant moments in Red Sox lore - Curt Schilling's courageous bloody sock game, Alex Rodriguez's slimy slap on Bronson Arroyo's glove and Johnny Damon's two home runs in Game Seven, one of which was a grand slam to pave the way for a surprisingly easy clinching-series game. As old farts like me would say, "it was one for the ages." For Boston fans, this felt like the US Olympic hockey team beating the Russians in Lake Placid (it didn't hurt that there were a bunch of Boston boys on that team, including Mike Eruzione). WE were the underdogs. WE were not projected to win. WE defied the odds.

Remember that the Red Sox-Yankees series only decided the American League representative in the World Series, the team that would face the St. Louis Cardinals. The Sox still needed to win another seven-game series to finally break the curse! The previous series was a monumental event in Boston sports history, this one almost felt like an afterthought. It wasn't much of a contest – after a Game One filled with lots of runs scored, the Red Sox starting pitchers (Martinez, Schilling, Lowe) in Games Two through Four were exceptional – each threw for at least six innings and their ERA was 0.00. I don't want to say that it was pre-determined that the Cardinals were going to lose, but you could almost sense the newly-forged resolve within the Sox. They had already overcome their biggest demon, the storied franchise that always, and I mean EVERY FREAKING TIME, beat them. But that wasn't true anymore. They were not that scared team anymore; the Yankees' bullying days were over. What's the other way to look at the Yankees' four-game losing streak? They choked; they couldn't seal the deal. I guess like a certain middle-aged guy who came out of the closet in his 40s, the Red Sox were late bloomers.

Sports Illustrated named the Boston Red Sox the '2004 Sportsman of the Year' (FYI – it's not just me, this was a BFD) and the emotional story about how New Englanders reacted to this historical moment was a beautiful amalgamation of triumph and sorrow. People wrote letters to the Red Sox, thanking them for finally winning, for finally extinguishing words like 'losers' and 'curse' and 'Babe Ruth.' The team was not prepared for such unusual requests – MANY fans wanted grave markers, something to give to friends and family who never got to see this day, some of whom may have never seen the team finally win. I bawled when I read this – I wanted my father to be here to share this with us. I know he gave up on baseball a decade earlier, but I also know that his heart would probably have melted when Boston finally won one over New York. My two older sisters love to watch baseball and golf, my triplet sister was a Division-1 athlete and we grew up playing sports year round in a sports-obsessed town. Loving the Red Sox is both nature and nurture in my family, and I wept when I thought about my dad missing that. I have no illusion that we would have shared a moment – he would have celebrated their championship with my brother or sister, it wouldn't be me, it was never me. The real reason that I cried was because I was sad about my father's sad life. Because I don't know what made him happy, whether he was ever truly happy with his life or his family, I wanted him to experience the sheer joy, mixed with a heavy dose of relief, of knowing for at least one year that the Red Sox came out on top. That we did it. That we were all a part of it.

Peter Leahy

Chapter Twelve

October 2015 – Mildred Sweet Mildred

My mother, born Mildred Mary Davis, had one joke about herself that she repeated quite often, "I'm so old I was a waitress at the Last Supper." What I'll always remember about her is that she saw the best in me – really that's what you want from any mother. I was a bright and curious kid and could read at an early age; she encouraged me to keep learning and discovering. She only attended high school but had a thirst for the unknown – she loved "In Search Of," an X-Files-related show from the 1970s that focused on paranormal phenomenon. She was fascinated by alternative medicines and as she gained weight as she got older, was always looking for the next miracle weight-loss cure.

That was a curious phenomenon – the triplets are naturally trim and athletic and my parents were heavy set, both had high blood pressure and were morbidly obese. It was simple – they were both sedentary and were likely eating their feelings of unhappiness. My father was always a bigger guy, so his beer belly (a loyal Schlitz man) was easy to hide. My mother was only 5'2" and was as skinny as my sisters when she was young and first married. We all get heavier as we get older, but for my mother, I can only assume it was the toll of essentially raising children by herself coupled with her loveless marriage that may have driven her to food as a form of solace. She owned A LOT of clothes, the majority of which she never wore and never took off the tags. Part of it was fluctuating weight and the other part of it was shopaholic-ish tendencies.

I believe that shopping replaced her primary responsibility for 20-odd years, raising the triplets – she "retired" when we all left for college. Of course she still worried and was involved in our lives and loved being a grandmother, but the four-bedroom house was empty; she was essentially out of a job. Raising the triplets was her mission, her ticket into heaven (let's be honest, with three hyper kids like me running around, she's up for sainthood). The children were also a buffer, a safe reason to not communicate with or try to salvage her marriage. I'm not blaming her; it appears that both parties had given up years ago.

Knowing what I know now, I think she lived vicariously through my youth and exuberance. She had achieved the ultimate success for a poor

Irish-Catholic girl from Boston – her children were living a much better life than her upbringing. She did not come from money and endured the Great Depression during her early years. She was a second-generation American and her parents had classic Irish names (Edward Davis and Catherine Shea) and all four of her grandparents were born in Ireland. The youngest of five children, she was seventeen years younger than the oldest, Helen. I love this story of when my mother was young; she couldn't pronounce the name Helen, so my mom called her "La La," and that is what everyone called her for 80+ years.

Her life before I came into existence remains a mystery, she rarely spoke of her past. She was most passionate about her mom - she wished that her mother was alive as she would have been thrilled to have triplets as grandbabies. When my parents were newlyweds, their first home was in a Northwestern suburb of Boston, next door to my mother's sister Mary and her husband Sam (I had an Uncle Sam – that still cracks me up) and their children. My grandmother would sometimes call and ask Milly what she was having for dinner (inviting herself) and if she didn't like the answer, she would call her other daughter to see if there was a better option!

When I came out to my mother, she asked two questions. The first, "Peetah, are you sure?" I replied yes. The second was "just tell me that you're not going to dress like a girl." And my response was "let me be clear, I'm bringing home a football player to you." That seemed to appease her, thinking that I had some type of bodyguard or protector. She also wanted to keep my reveal within the immediate family, which lasted about a week.

She knew I was unhappily married for years – my weekend rituals were the same: stay home with the children and clean the house while my wife was out shopping. I would call her most Saturdays and share stories about the children and avoid talking about my marriage. About four years before my big announcement, I was on the phone with her when my wife came home. I didn't end the call correctly and my mother heard her yelling at me, belittling me and complaining about everything. My mom had evidence of what was going on with me, but she said nothing. That's how she was raised – we don't air our dirty laundry to the public. I wonder if she was surprised and maybe ashamed that my marriage was as unfulfilling as hers?

When I started typing these stories, I knew that many of my experiences and issues were influenced by my upbringing, and that I was repeating patterns. I knew that I was like my father in more ways than I care to admit but it's just dawning on me that I have so much of my mother in me – sacrificing my happiness for the sake of my children, staying in a relationship with a person that you no longer recognize. My first marriage and the one that my parents endured were flawed for different reasons (mine has a lot to do with the title of this book), but the parallels are scary:

- ✓ Staying together for the children – easily the most popular excuse to be with someone you don't love. You create this magical theory that you are properly raising healthy children by staying together until they graduate high school, then you can finally end your responsibility, be free and be with someone who truly makes you happy.
- ✓ Becoming a parent and losing your identity – I don't know what my parents did for fun before they got married or at least before the triplets were born, but I rarely saw them smile when they were together. They were serious about parenting and focused on their children, but I saw little joy in either of them. I never knew the importance of truly being happy and in love – that's the behavior that you want to model for your children, the legacy that you want to pass down.
- ✓ Roommates / ships passing in the night – my parents also slept in separate beds (admittedly, it was my father's thunderous snoring) and when he retired, their Golden Years consisted of them living on separate floors of the house. My favorite crazy/sad story is that my mother primarily lived on the main floor with cable tv and the home phone. My father purchased a cell phone and connected DirectTV to the bedroom television so that he didn't have to be in the same room with her.
- ✓ Using the children as a weapon on your spouse – I've shared how our mother insidiously drove us to hate our father and similarly, I'll never forget the time that my wife casually made a joke to our daughter, "make sure you don't marry a man like your father." Or the time my daughter came out as I was mowing the front yard to tell me that I was 'scorching the lawn.' I didn't respond on either occasion but wish I had. I don't want my daughter to become a bully in her relationships and similarly, I will feel horrible if my son becomes a pushover in his relationship. That's my biggest fear about my children and their relationships, that they repeat our mistakes.

If I'm looking at my parents fairly, I have to categorically state that my father was not a monster and my mother was not a saint. I have forgiven my father, but I'm not sure if I'm ready to absolve my mother for the way that she treated her husband and turned his children against him. (*Paging Doctor Freud – is Peter talking about his mother or his ex-wife, will we ever know?*). Yes, it appears that I was involved in the same dysfunctional family dynamic as my parents. I used the word involved, as in the past, and I need to remind myself almost daily that that unhealthy relationship doesn't exist anymore. Getting out of the marriage was about breaking the cycle, changing the rules and shifting the paradigm – however you want to say that I'm not living in the past defensively. I pivoted and am actively creating and owning my future.

My mother's last gift to me came in 2015 after her death. She sold her mortgage-free family home at full price with no inspection before entering assisted living and after she passed, she divided those proceeds among her five children. I was able to use those monies as a down payment for my current home, my first major purchase since the bankruptcy discharge and the short sale. Let's be honest, if I was still married to my wife when I received my mother's estate, it would be spent. It would be gone and we would have nothing tangible to show for it.

She died on a Sunday in October – it was Atlanta Pride weekend and I was all excited about marching in the parade with other gay fathers. If you've never been to a pride festival, it is fun and beautiful arrangement of colors. These events have become more 'professional' as more companies become involved and show their support of the LGBTQ+ community – that's not a bad thing, just a reality of where we are today. For all of the corporate representation, this is still an area where people fly their freak flag and dress in all kinds of provocative outfits and costumes. When I'm not parading around with the dads, I'm working for my company, so I'm wearing something corporate pride-ish. I helped out at the 2019 Pride festival in Augusta Georgia and I was told to wear my company shirt and something with rainbows. I nailed it (see below) and this was the first time that I had ever been stopped for photo ops – people wanted their picture with me! You don't have to guess – I already owned that entire ensemble.

Chapter Thirteen

December 2014 - Dating in the 21st Century + Gay Apps – What the Heck is Going On?

2014 was the first year that I finally lived as my authentic self. At the end of the year I reflected on some of my accomplishments and memorable moments:

- ✓ I took control of my life, owned my "go to" passive-aggressive behavior (victimhood) – I stopped being that old Peter
- ✓ Loved people, things and experiences with all my heart – I told people that I loved them and I meant it
- ✓ Lived passionately, no longer driven by fear
- ✓ Celebrated my birthday for the first time in over a decade
- ✓ Had my first boy crush, and my first semi-boyfriend, and met another guy that I thought was super - all of them had some great qualities; meeting those guys helped me better understand the man that I am becoming, as well as what my ideal partner will look like
- ✓ Went to my first Bear Run & Gay Beach (Pensacola)
- ✓ Took my kids on an amazing Orlando vacation
- ✓ Traveled for pleasure to Montreal, St. Louis and Panama City Beach, Florida
- ✓ Learned that I love clothes, decorating and cooking
- ✓ Lowered my cholesterol and blood pressure through diet and exercise after both were suddenly elevated (stress and poor diet)
- ✓ Learned to be a good friend, to support and love those I care about
- ✓ Met many Gay Fathers - awesome fellowship!
- ✓ Went to Boston for a family reunion - got the triplets together for the first time in 11 years

Late 2014/early 2015 was a time of transition – an opportunity for me to get serious about someone. I felt ready and more secure about myself. I was still holding on to some heavy emotional baggage relating to my father and my ex-wife, but I was aware of my need for growth, I was prepared to deal with it and I wanted someone special to help me grow, for us to build a life together. Semi-recently out of the closet and looking for men to date – sounds easy, right? To put it into perspective, the last time I attempted to woo someone, Ronald Regan was still the president – YIKES! It's a weird feeling, to be fresh on the dating scene and not a spring chicken. Plus I don't know any of the rules for dating in the gay world and I'm not sure what other guys are looking for. For a long time I was worried that I would be viewed as damaged goods. I'm certainly not the first man to come out of the closet later in life, but it was obvious that I was still discovering who I was, what I wanted for myself and in a relationship and what I needed in my next partner.

As opposed to learning as I go (I was a DIY Gay!) I should have started with the Five W's – WHO are these beefy bears that I'm seeing in bars or on dating-hookup apps. WHERE are they – is any type of relationship realistic if he's more than 50 miles away. WHAT is he looking for – is he looking for a monogamous relationship, do we share similar values? WHEN is he ready to settle down – does he want something permanent and is he comfortable with a guy who may not fully understand himself and has not yet been in a serious gay relationship? Most importantly, WHY are they online, are they single or are they an "it's complicated" couple? Being online allows you to lie about anything – are you cheating on your partner, what do you look like (carefully edited photo, pictures from 10-15 years ago) or your photos may not even be you – catfishing exists everywhere.

You've heard of Tinder, Match and Bumble – well it's time you meet their gay male cousins: Grindr, Scruff and GROWLr. Please tell me that I don't have to explain Grindr to you – yes it's a hookup app, yes guys are probably just looking for sex and nothing else. They may be married to a man or a woman and you may never learn their real name. You shouldn't be shocked – throughout history there have been thousands, if not millions of examples of people going home with someone that they just met in a bar. Remove the bar, add a phone + GPS, and voila! The new "how to get lucky quickly" option. Scruff is like Grindr, but it's all about body and facial hair – you can't fake attraction and there's a market out there for guys that have hairy bodies and those that like that in others. I call it Hirsute Pursuit.

GROWLr was the only app that I had on my phone and it suited me perfectly. Spoiler Alert: this app is for Bears, Bears that like Bears and Bears that like Chasers. As soon as I downloaded it and created my profile, I was hooked (pun intended). Like other dating apps, you can see people that are currently online globally as well as who's in your local area. I was single and ready to mingle, but I also wanted something deeper, something real. I spent a lot of time writing my profile – who I was, my interests and what was important to me. If you looked up "Slim Snuggler" (yes that was my name!!), you would have read:

Enjoy all forms of touch for affection - snuggling, cuddling, spooning, falling asleep in beefy and hairy arms that make me feel warm-safe-protected. I am a cuddle cub.

Big into reading (mysteries, thrillers), movies, music, and trivia and bigger Boston sports fan! Love watching pro football, basketball and baseball. Follow many liberal political blogs. Love being outdoors, viewing historical sites, museums, botanical gardens and shopping for bargains. Roller coasters & water parks, yeah! Cry at most Pixar movies. Animal lover - believe in adoption. Learning to cook and love it! DDF (NOTE: disease and drug-free). Non-smoker, social drinker – love me a Spicy Bloody Mary.

To better understand me:

Music - Beatles, Classic Rock, Power Pop, Mash-Ups; Movies - Spinal Tap, original Star Wars, Action, Mystery, Thriller; Comedy - Steven Wright and Stephen Lynch; Radio - NPR, especially Wait, Wait Don't Tell Me; TV - Arrested Development, Lost, Sherlock, Archer; Personality - Humor (twisted, ability to laugh at self) is huge with me; Food - Anything spicy & messy, sushi, chocolate

47 years on the planet, Gemini. 5'10", 170 lbs. - fairly active and trim.

Value my friends and the joy they bring to my life - not afraid to say 'I Love You' to those that have my best interest in mind.

My perfect day involves something like visiting historical sites/ nature walk, followed by cooking dinner together (I'll cook, you clean), snuggling on the couch for a movie/TV/sports, then dessert in bed.

I met my first boyfriend Jeffrey on GROWLr. He lived in Miami and taught Portuguese and Queer Studies at a major university. Within weeks we were texting and FaceTiming and I visited him for the weekend in the last week of January 2015 (coincidently, Super Bowl Sunday, New England Patriots vs. Seattle Seahawks). I was excited to finally meet in person and looking forward to spending quality time together, plus I had never visited the Sunshine State as a gay man. I was nervous about meeting Jeffrey's ex-partner. Even though they were no longer a couple, they were still active in each other's lives, including taking cruises together. They lived together in a small one-bedroom apartment in South Beach. Yes it was one bedroom…with one bed. They slept in the same bed. Yes I was weirded out when I learned that.

This example of two guys that are no longer a couple but live together out of convenience or financial security or because they don't want to be alone happens quite frequently in the gay community. It mirrors something else that is common – open relationships. It is accepted that many couples open up their sexual relationship and the variations are plenty – they may 'play' (code word for fooling around / having sex) together or separately. It's not my place to judge, people are free to decide their household rules. Unfortunately, you find all too often that when someone says that they're in an open relationship, they're actually cheating on their partner or husband. Remember that when you're on an app, you don't need to use your real name and you can travel outside the home to fool around. It's a telltale sign that when a guy cannot host or wants you to visit him, there is some type of deception with his other half.

When I met Jeffery's ex-partner, he went from hero to zero in minutes. I understood why he was single; he was so arrogant and he loved bossing Jeffrey around. I swear I was experiencing transference, right away I felt the need to protect and defend Jeffrey in front of his aggressor. The ex-partner made no bones that he was the boss when the two of them were together and unfortunately, Jeffrey did nothing to change that dynamic. I was so giddy when I finally learned that that guy was a raging asshole!

The weekend in Miami was magical – we watched the sunrise on the beach on Saturday morning, we walked along Collins Avenue and soaked up the South Beach atmosphere and I ate foods from around the world – I tried Peruvian and Argentinian foods for the first time. Sunday was even better – we met one of my work girlfriends in Hollywood and walked along the Broadwalk. Then we watched the Super Bowl with another bear buddy of mine at Rosie's Bar & Grill in Wilton Manors. Wilton Manors (Jeffrey called it Wilted Manhood) is the San Francisco and Provincetown of South Florida – a significant number of LGBTQ+ people live there and every bar, restaurant and shop is LGBTQ+ friendly.

The weekend was picture-perfect in several ways - I could be myself here and there was no one from my past that would "out" me. We're way past the divorce and the second lawsuit, but I was still a work in progress.

Jeffrey and I realistically dated for about four months – we were 'together' for longer than that, but he was slowly ghosting me as we saw each other less often, as he failed to return my calls. During that brief period, I was beaming with pride that I could tell my gay friends that I had someone special. One of the sweetest things that I remember was keeping a notepad at my desk and cataloging 'stories' that I would share later when we called for our nightly check-in. I got to truly know him intimately for a moment in time and similarly, he was an important part of my life. My mother's birthday was in June and I asked him to send a birthday card to her in her nursing home. He did and he told her that he was crazy about her son. That summer I went to visit my mom up in Massachusetts and we FaceTimed Jeffrey. I will always be appreciative of how sweet he was to her. My mom died about four months after that call and she finally saw me happy. I pray that it might have given her a sense of peace.

Even though we were no longer an active couple, Jeffrey and I had already booked a Caribbean cruise together during Thanksgiving. Jeffrey's ex-partner was in the travel industry and he worked some magic to upgrade our room – it was a sweet gesture. The ex-partner was seeing someone at the time and we had planned for the four of us to go together. Well they broke up and the ex-partner didn't want to spend the money for the entire room, so he didn't accompany us. Later I found out that Jeffrey was willing to compensate for the missing person – which completely broke my heart. Jeffrey knew how I felt about his ex-partner and if he was willing to spend money to ensure that this other guy could attend, essentially ruining our time together, then he made his priorities pretty clear.

I mentioned that we were no longer an active couple, but the cruise brought some of that magic back. We were together 24/7, there were no cell phones or other distractions and we were always busy with some type of activity (eating, drinking, spa, watching movies in the pool). One night I had an emotional double-feature: I watched the New England Patriots win a game with a bunch of other Boston sports fans then Jeffrey and I watched the Sound of Music together, a film that makes me cry multiple times, every time.

It was tempting to see if we could rekindle our relationship, but I was worried. I did something on the last night of the cruise that I'm not proud of. After Jeffrey fell asleep, I sat up in bed and unlocked his phone. I was not surprised by what I read for the next two to three hours. Jeffrey was madly in love with someone in The Netherlands who was already married to another man and was communicating with him throughout the whole trip, professing his love for this guy and sending him photos from our cruise, including pictures of him that I had taken! I think I slept for about 30 minutes that night. I knew it was over, there was no going back from this, but I was still dumbfounded and just plain sad. I never told him what I knew, that he was already working on his next conquest.

I was back to work the next Monday after the cruise and I officially broke it off with him. I told him that I couldn't do this anymore, I wanted to be with someone who truly wanted me. His reply, "I knew this was going to happen, you were always too good for me." I responded angrily, "don't give me that bullshit, I fucking chose you." I didn't say that to sound arrogant, I meant that I invested my whole heart in him. I liked him, maybe even loved him, for all of his faults and I wanted him. I wanted us to be a happy couple.

I think fondly of Jeffrey and I wish him happiness when he eventually finds a partner. He's like a lot of us – attempting to escape from his past and in many ways broken. I knew what I was getting when we first started chatting, he admitted to me that he didn't believe in marriage (he called it "heteronormative") and guess what I did? I convinced myself that I could change him, that I was special enough for him to change into the person that I wanted him to be. It was a significant learning experience – I didn't get hurt, but it provided another glimpse of what I wanted in a relationship. I wanted honesty, communication, affection and most importantly, trust.

Chapter Fourteen

July 2013 - Going to Provincetown, Finding Gay Bear Mecca

Within 30 days of separating from my wife I had the opportunity to attend Bear Week in Provincetown, Massachusetts. For those of you who don't know Ptown, it's a LGBTQ+-friendly town at the very tip of Cape Cod and Bear Week is one of their largest tourism weeks of the year. Every July over nine days and nights about 10,000 tourists descend into this town of 3,000 permanent residents. I've been multiple times and we've always lucked out with great weather. It's a place to see bears of all shapes and sizes and it's also the place <u>TO BE SEEN</u>. As you walk down Commercial Street or attend a Tea Dance or a themed costume party, you'll see guys with outfits that may include a combination of tiny-flashy-sparkly-leather and everything in between.

My first time was with Dave – he had a small condo and was a part-time resident. That weekend was the last time I saw him and I had a horrible time, but he holds a special place in my heart because of the role that he played in giving me the courage to leave my wife. We e-mailed back and forth (this was before texting was a thing) for a few months before I finally got the courage to leave her. Before my HR friend and Joy helped me break out of my shell, he was my emotional support. Again, we only "knew" each other for maybe 2-3 months, but he was my backbone when I was so meek and tentative. I saw Dave right before I confronted my wife and he did something to me – something that I always wanted but was so afraid of. He shaved my head – he made me Lex Luthor bald! For years I was riddled with insecurity around my thinning hair and bald spot – it was another part of me that didn't work, that I didn't like about myself. I would not have been able to leave her without Dave's support and similarly, I didn't have the balls to shave my head.

When I was with my wife, getting my hair cut was a significant issue between us. No lie – I had to beg her to do it, there was usually something more important to her, normally a television show. We didn't have any disposable income and because my hair looked like crap (that's how I saw myself, as a steaming pile of dogshit), why not save money and cut it at home? There never seemed to be a right time, I remember hesitating and/or trying to locate a good mood opportunity for me to ask. During the many years that she was trimming my head every 4-6 weeks, I said on more than one occasion, "do you think I should shave my head?" She always responded firmly, stating "don't do that, you have an oddly shaped head." And I like a dummy, I believed her.

I held my breath when Dave used the trimmer on my head and when he was done I felt like an alien. I didn't know that Peter – I had such beautiful dirty blonde hair growing up and now I willingly removed it. Seeing myself in the mirror I was looking at a new Peter, like a snake sloughing off its skin, I was reborn. I need to emphasize that there were two emotions building inside of me – the development of a new Peter and the discarding of the old me. Look at the before and after – these are my official corporate photos, 2006 vs. 2018. I swear I look twelve years YOUNGER in the after photo!

I flew to Boston that July, took the ferry to Provincetown and I was filled with amazement and wonder. I was going to be around the largest amount of gay men – ALL BEARS – that I had ever seen. I got off the boat and knew no one – nobody that would know my history, my insecurities. I was walking into an environment where being gay was normal - no apologizing, no excuses, no explaining. No thinking, all being. Going to events like these (Bear Run, Bear Week, Bear Cruises) centers around people that are like-minded souls and don't have to make any conscious decisions about places to go or people to talk to, for fear that there might be some kind of backlash. Because I spent the majority of my adult life pretending to be straight, I never had to navigate whether an environment was LGBTQ+-friendly or not. Coming out of the closet and announcing to the world that you belonged to a minority and sometimes persecuted group is an eye-opening experience. You realize how much you take for granted when you are white and presumably straight, nearly all doors open for you. For others that look or act different, like skin color or disability, they usually have to work harder or be smarter to be afforded the same opportunities.

My long weekend in Provincetown was not that fantastic, it was rather boring - a major letdown. We went to the community pool once (I didn't own any Speedos yet), but most nights we had dinner at his place – we didn't go out dancing at the disco bar or soak in the party-like atmosphere that happens every night. And Dave's place – that is a story! I didn't know much about him when I accepted his P-town invitation and when I arrived, I was confronted with the reality that he was a hoarder. There was a tiny pathway to navigate from the front door to the kitchen to upstairs, but otherwise there was no livable space. Despite being over 50 years old, as far as I knew, Dave had never held a full-time job (his wealthy parents owned a couple of shopping malls) and his place reflected his wayward lifestyle.

I bought a Provincetown t-shirt during the trip and it represents where my head was at the time – it was grey (not a bold color or even remotely gay) and size large - I had not yet embraced that I had a tiny frame and could look good in size medium. It was fun and such a relief to BE gay somewhere else because when I came home to my wife and my children and my co-workers, the fabulous side of me went back into the closet – I wasn't ready to be one whole person. That was the primary issue when I started to go to therapy after leaving her. I spent so much energy pretending to be different people to different audiences, I was mentally exhausted. It's no surprise that I needed that week-long mental vacation a month before Provincetown. I wasn't a completely healed person yet.

I went back to Provincetown three years later – I was a different person and fully immersed myself in Bear Week. I caught on pretty quickly to a typical schedule:

9:00 - 10:00 am	Out for breakfast, depending on how late you were out the night before
12:00	Enjoy (and more importantly be seen) at the Provincetown Inn pool
3:00	Disco Nap (yes, this is a real term, essentially you're gearing up for a long night and/or making up for not enough sleep from last night)
4:00	Tea Dance - usually a theme –time for a costume change!
8:00	Dinner
9:00 - 10:00 pm	If you're not attending a show or comedy club, you hit the bar or club; there's a different theme every night (white party, underwear party, fetish night, etc.) so you better be prepared for another costume change
12:00 am	Get some pizza and eat outside while you recap the night and people watch

That was pretty much my routine and it was a treat to enjoy that experience and share it with friends. The picture below was taken just after a Tea Dance - check out that FANTASTIC lighting at 7:52 pm and I just love my expression – pure joy. And did you notice my blue toenails? Painting my nails every summer is now a sweet tradition that my husband and I share. I love to add color, to be goofy and silly and most importantly, to have the confidence to not care what other people think.

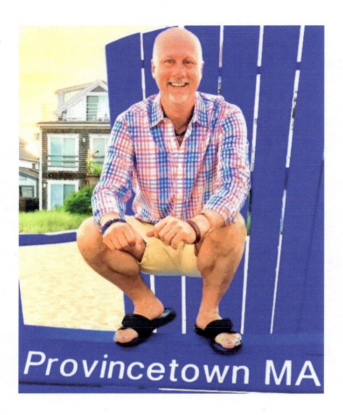

I mentioned that I enjoyed Bear Week with friends. During that week I met so many people that I knew online and it was beautiful to finally meet them in person and cement our friendships. I was overwhelmed with delight when I finally got to have a drink and dance and to receive a hug from them (Spoiler Alert: I abso-fucking-lutely love to be hugged!). I told them that I loved them and I meant it and it was real. Three years prior, my Bear Week experience was tentative and awkward, this time I came as a fully realized gay man. I was proud of who I was and my multiple tight and tiny outfits reflected that. I wanted to see people and I wanted to be seen. I wanted to catch up with online friends and make new friends and have a great time.

Chapter Fifteen

September 2013 - Unlocking a New Passion, Creatively Cooking for Health

Living on my own for the first time in my life at age 45 was a respite from my chaotic and stressful life with my ex-wife. I did see my children every morning as I drove them to school, but most nights it was just me. I was learning to be comfortable being alone, to reset and find out what I truly valued, what was important to me and how I wanted to spend my time. Pretty quickly I found out that I enjoyed eating a whole frozen pizza every night – one of my faves was the Freshetta® Naturally Rising Crust Canadian Style Bacon & Pineapple Pizza. If you eat all of it in one sitting (I don't recommend it), you're taking in 1,740 calories and a whopping 4,080 milligrams of sodium.

Despite my constant stress in the last dozen or so years of my marriage, my vital signs had been consistent – textbook-perfect blood pressure and average cholesterol levels. A few months after living on my own and I was shocked to learn that my blood pressure was high and my cholesterol increased by over 50 points. I remember telling my doctor, "really, I've never been happier in my life!" It's funny now to think that I couldn't see how my unhealthy eating was reversing all of the good that I was doing. I needed to make a change. It was time to learn to cook.

My mother was not a whiz in the kitchen, God love her. She was crazy busy and I recall having some type of a casserole every night. Now I romanticize these meals, mainly because we all ate together, minus my dad, in a world before cell phones and other technologies that rule our lives. This was the regular meal rotation – let's see if you grew up with:

- American Chop Suey - ground beef, stewed tomatoes, elbow macaroni
- Hungarian Goulash – ground beef, chopped celery, topped with La Choy Chinese noodles
- Tuna Noodle Casserole – tuna, wide egg noodles and peas topped with crushed Wise's potato chips
- Chicken & Rice Bake – chicken pieces, cream of mushroom soup, Minute rice

- Spaghetti and Meat Sauce – if you grew up in Boston, you know that Wednesday is "Prince Spaghetti Day"

When I married my wife, she did most of the cooking. She didn't have a signature dish, but I don't recall that anything was particularly horrible. I ate what was presented to me and didn't complain. When I finally started to cook I quickly realized that she wasn't cooking / making something, she was only reheating. A 'fancy' meal for the family was rotisserie chicken, prepacked green beans sauteed in olive oil, premade mashed potatoes from the refrigerated section and Pillsbury crescent rolls. When I think about what I ate then versus what I eat now, my former life was like Dorothy in Kansas (bland menu, black & white world) and the Journey to Oz represents my new culinary pallet (spices, colors, exploring new flavors and cultures).

You have to start somewhere and luckily my local supermarket consistently created easy-to-follow recipes that allowed me to try new foods or offered a twist on a traditional recipe. I'll never forget "Kickin' Peach Chicken," a chicken breast that is marinated in peach preserves and Sriracha sauce, definitely sweet and spicy! Cooking quickly evolved into a creative outlet – not only did I savor making a flavorful dinner, but I loved trying out new desserts and sharing them with my co-workers.

One of my finest creations – carrot cake with shredded carrots, raisins and crushed pineapple topped with a cream cheese frosting with added coconut, walnuts, and orange zest. I surprised my team with something delicious about 2-3 times a month – I didn't need an occasion – and that became part of my new workplace identity. I was 'dessert guy' and reveled in the joy that I was bringing. Other co-workers treated the office to something homemade and more often than not, they thought it came from me!

I was cooking to eat healthier foods and as an outlet for creativity; and slowly I realized I was cooking for love. I adore inventing something new or with color or a unique flavor combination – ideally all three! This was the new me, Chef Peter was born. The Food Network has plenty of celebrity cooking shows and competitions, there's always something to learn. I didn't realize it at first, but I was becoming a student and learning a new language. When talking to someone else about their recent creation I asked them to walk me through the recipe in a step-by-step process. I would close my eyes and visualize myself in my kitchen; Would I want to make this? Could I tailor the recipe to align with my preferences? Should I make this if I wanted to impress a guy with a meal?

I realized that I had a knack for cooking and I had my cholesterol and blood pressure under control and I'm exercising semi-regularly, but I wasn't losing weight, I was slowly getting thick in the middle. Like many middle-aged men, I was pencil thin when I graduated from high school (150 lbs.) and as I entered my late 40's, my 170-ish weight turned into 180 then 190 – I hit a peak at 194. Something had to change – I had to do something different and drastic. I mentioned that I loved my skinny body in tight outfits, but the growing love handles and mini pouch upfront were not my best look.

Coincidently, my workplace created a healthy challenge competition – pay an entry fee and see if you can lose 10 pounds in 10 weeks. I opted in as I had nothing to lose - this time that is NOT a pun. I enjoyed exercising during most lunch hours (it's all about the music, I'll explain later) but this time I decided to also change my diet. I went low carb, removing all bread, pasta and potatoes. Per the rules of the contest, you hopped on the scale weekly and if you maintained your weight or if the number went up, you added money to the pot that would be divided among the contest winners. Yours truly was the number one Biggest

Loser – seventeen pounds over ten weeks – I lost twenty-five pounds in total. These photos were taken three months apart – you can see the weight loss around my eyes and my chin. And before you ask, the photo on the right was our Christmas Ugly Sweater contest. I purchased that women's vest at a thrift store for $5.05 and it won me first prize and a cool $50.00!

There was a curious benefit to altering my diet. You may not know this, but men of a certain age often wake up in the middle of the night because they need to urinate - I rarely sleep straight through the night anymore. Before my low-carb lifestyle, I had the same ritual: get up around 4:00 am and after I hit the bathroom, I would walk to the kitchen for some Greek yogurt. I normally woke up with a sour stomach and needed something to lower the acidic feeling, to cool the temperature. The yogurt did the trick and I didn't question why I needed it, I thought it was normal. Flash forward to the new Low Carb Peter and that went away – it's like the gluten was affecting me in ways that I didn't realize.

I normally downplay my weight loss success. I try not to pat myself on the back around others and I often use self-deprecating humor, something like "if I knew this diet was going to be so successful, I would have done it 10-20 years ago!" As you can already tell from my multiple stories, it's not about the food. Having fun while cooking and enjoying what I eat and creating something new and tasty for friends is about living in the moment. Food is an extension of how I feel about you; how comfortable I am in my skin. It's about creating memories. I take photos of every meal I create and that's another side of me, the picture taker. Most of the time I don't share them on social media – it's not for others, it's for me. I'll go into more in the next chapter, but capturing these moments is important – I want to celebrate the little things in life: to remember people, scenes and memories from today as well as my childhood. I feel like I'm still compensating, still making up for lost time.

Chapter Sixteen

27,200+ Snapshots of a Life Well Lived and my 'Cerebral Music'

When I was first married, our nightlife was predictable and boring. After we put the children to bed, my wife settled in the den to watch television and I went upstairs to play on the computer. Why did we not spend any quality time together? Let's be honest - we didn't enjoy each other's company and our den had only a love seat, so only one adult could fit. Television was her escape. I believe she viewed it as her time, there were no demands from her husband or children. Her sleeping schedule was unique, dare I say unhealthy - this was her daily routine:

5:30 am	Wake up, get ready for school, she has to be there by 7:05 am
3:30 pm	Leave school with the children
4:00 pm	Two-hour afternoon nap, she wakes up when I get home
6:00 pm	Prepare dinner, help children with homework and bedtime rituals
9:00 pm	TV time
Midnight	Bedtime

I went to bed around 10:30 or 11:00 each night and started my day around 6:30. It was easy for us to have separate schedules – we were essentially roommates who happened to have children together and more importantly, we hadn't slept in the same bed in over 10 years.

With my computer time I pursued two of my passions – pictures and music. Like many young parents, we had tons of photos of the children, but over time there were fewer ones of me, and almost none of us as a couple or a family. We were given digital photo frames at work and I quickly realized that many of the kid's photos could be saved to a thumb drive and I could 'see' them all day at my work. I was alone almost every night (zero friends and no social life!), so I started collecting other images that were important to me – pictures of my hometown, Boston sports, Classic Rock albums, funny Internet memes – really anything that made me smile, anything that defined my personality. Most of the collection represented something from my past or something that I was observing from afar. Nothing reflected me – no unique experiences, no fun times with friends, no memories worth keeping or sharing.

Like many people in 2022, my phone is my camera and I love to take pictures and be in pictures that forever capture a moment. Coming out and being happy and having friends and being goofy is the real me and I love how a photo can take me back to a moment and the emotions and good times that come with it. I'm happy that I flipped the script – for about five years, my photo collection represented me barely participating in life from the sidelines. As I now live and love fearlessly, I take photos with my friends and I'm very upfront about it – I tell them that pictures are important to me and I love you and when we're not together in person, I want the opportunity to see you and think of you fondly. I guess I can be a little aggressive sometimes (I NEED my photographer to hold the phone up high to minimize a potential double chin) and I'm not asking for their permission – this is who I am, this is what I love doing. I see pictures on your phone as a photo album that's stuck in a drawer – hidden and not enjoyed. That's why I transfer photos to my frame and hence my 27,000+ collection. I continue to constantly expand my collection – about 60-70% of those photos were added over the past five years. I am growing as a person and am open to new experiences and friends. When I log onto my computer with my coffee and hazelnut creamer and Fiber One Chocolate Peanut Butter protein bar, turning on my digital frame is integral to my morning ritual. It makes me smile every minute of every hour of every workday. It sparks my creativity too, keeps my mind occupied and helps the time go faster. It's also a great distraction when conference calls go long.

The growing photo collection is not just me and my husband (for the record, I have AT LEAST 1,110 photos of him or us together). There are photos of gay father friends and their children, plus other friends that are smiling with their fur babies. I care about my chosen family and what's important to them - I am actively supporting them as I'm celebrating my new life. I am wary about oversharing too much of myself on social media (yes that's ironic as I've written twenty-odd chapters of my personal history and struggles), my pictures are MINE - a gift I keep giving to myself.

My music collection of 6,000+ songs represents another labor of love, a well-nurtured collection of Beatles-esque Power Pop, Classic Rock, everything 80's, mashups and early 90's alternative rock. It was iTunes and the introduction of the iPod and amazingly, my local public library that helped me craft this assortment. You know that we were living beyond our means and relied on financial trickery to live month-to-month. Money was tight, so I couldn't afford to buy CDs or download songs. But a library card is free! Over 8-9 years, I scoured the libraries of Aurora and Naperville, Illinois (2004-2006) and Cumming-Alpharetta-Roswell, Georgia (2006-2013) to check out CDs, download select songs and expand my musical horizons.

I'm super happy with this collection – I rarely add songs now (too busy living my best life), but at the time, that was my source of fun. Creating the collection was a lonely activity, but I needed something to pass the time. For many years I was alone inside my head and I guess music was a way to not feel so isolated. Similar to my wife's devotion to television, the rest of my unhappy and pathetic life temporarily disappeared when I lost myself in the latest earworm that tickled my fancy.

Music will always be a passion – it's not just listening, it's the background information (aka trivia) that enhances my love. I love reading, collecting random facts and sharing them with friends (and let's be honest – to win at trivia contests too). I have some 'Cliff Claven' in me (the postman from the television show Cheers who was full of random knowledge and devoid of a personality), but I guess I see it as an opportunity to continually learn and discover.

There was always music playing in our home growing up, and it's pretty comical how we all got along because nobody enjoyed the same style of music. My father loved Arthur Fiedler and the Boston Pops and quite curiously, university marching bands. Yes, this is a genre of music and our living room high-fi played these albums again and again. For my mother it was Frank Sinatra, Tony Bennett and Engelbert Humperdink - all crooners. She couldn't get enough of Glenn Miller, Tommy Dorsey and the Big Band era. My parents didn't listen to each other's music, but they peacefully co-existed – an apt metaphor for their 'staying together for the children' marriage.

My older sisters were avid record (and 8-track tape!) collectors in the 1970s and I am forever grateful for their Classic Rock influence and education. Back when you listened to an entire album in one sitting and the album art was part of the overall packaging, I was fascinated. I'm going to go all "OK Boomer" on you right now, but many of these albums are pretty fucking perfect and the music of today pretty much sucks: Fleetwood Mac, Rumours; Steely Dan, Aja; Elton John, Goodbye Yellow Brick Road; Boz Skaggs, Silk Degrees; Steve Miller, Book of Dreams; Eagles, Hotel California and Jackson Brown, Running on Empty. They also loved Boston and Foreigner and the Doobie Brothers and anything that represented Album Oriented Rock from 1973-1979. They were generous about sharing their collection with us and eventually, I started to build my record collection – my first two purchases were Supertramp's Breakfast in America and The Cars debut album.

Fleetwood Mac's Rumors album was the one album (it wasn't just the album – at some point we owned the album, 8-track tape, cassette tape and the CD) that spoke to us, listening to that was a shared family experience. I mentioned that my mother didn't get her driver's license until she was 50 and her first car was a 1974 yellow Chevy Nova with an 8-track player. The car represented her independence and Rumors was its official soundtrack. It's funny to think about a record that was fueled by two couples breaking up and a band taking an insane number of drugs became the vehicle for our family to listen together in peace – no fighting was allowed when it played.

My oldest sister took me to my first concert in 1983 (The Police, A Flock of Seagulls, the Fixx) and not surprisingly, it was the first time that I smelled marijuana. What shocks me about this event was how generous she was. She was in her early 20s and her siblings were nine years younger than her, barely teenagers. That's pretty damn cool that she made time for us to have this experience.

The triplets went in different directions musically – for my sister it was all Whitney Houston and Madonna and anything that you might hear on a KISS radio station. With time I have come to appreciate Whitney's once-in-a-lifetime vocal talents and how Madonna has evolved into a music icon, but back then her musical choices were an extension of disco, which was "not cool". My brother's musical collection started with mostly classic rock (Eric Clapton, Bob Dylan, Traffic, AC/DC.) but then he took a weird turn with 80's hair metal bands like Ratt, Dokken, Motley Crew and Poison. I went through a couple of phases – alternative (Devo, Violent Femmes, Yaz), classic rock (I saw Boston, Billy Joel, Bob Seger in concert) and then I discovered Rush. For some reason this Canadian power trio took a hold of me and I was obsessed for years. I loved their advanced musicianship and obtuse lyrics. Rush is one of those bands that you get or you don't. I'm not pretending to be some kind of a music snob (I'm looking at you, jazz aficionados!), their music just spoke to me. I can see how an outsider might not understand the band's appeal - the lead singer's voice can be grating and their lyrical content can be seen as cold and unemotional. My high school friend Oliver summed it up best, he said "Rush has no soul." Ouch!

Listening to music and memorizing lyrics/song & album statistics are only part of my musical condition. There is always a song playing in my head – my high school roommate called it "Cerebral Music." For some reason my brain stores memories through a music-based lens. It's like the music frames the picture and sets the emotional tone. In addition to keeping myself occupied, I often share song facts that I find interesting (my friends would say random).

The rest of my body follows suit – from singing off key (both lead and background vocals) to air guitar to acting out various drum solos, I'm immersed in every song. Music is my escape (methinks it might be my excuse) during exercise. It works for me, passing the time as I pretend to be on stage. Do I look goofy and perhaps a bit awkward? You bet I do. I do admit that it can be weird when I start singing in the supermarket – if you see some random guy singing "My Sharonna" down the cereal aisle, are you going to strike up a conversation? Of course you aren't. When I'm in my music zone, I don't see other people and don't care what they think about me. Every part of me is beaming with joy and I'm not looking for anyone's approval as I'm singing and sashaying!

My son did not inherit the music gene – I don't think he has a favorite band or uses a streaming service – but my daughter is a music-aholic. When she was younger, two incidents made me beam with pride (I'm sure she has forgotten them). The first one included the 2008 song "All Summer Long" from Kid Rock. His lyrics are combined with a musical mash-up, combining Werewolves of London from Warren Zevon and Sweet Home Alabama from Lynyrd Skynyrd. She's 5-6 years old and she 'hears' the Sweet Home Alabama guitar riff. I nearly jumped out of my seat – she is correctly identifying the music and she was exhibiting a weird musical talent like her goofy dad. I was so damn happy that I was rubbing off on her, like I was helping complete her Jedi training.

The second one occurred when she was around eleven, she shared that she loved both AC/DC and Nirvana. I was overcome with joy! I couldn't wait to tell her about Nirvana's Nevermind album as a seminal moment in music history and the onset of grunge and the end of hair metal. Similarly, AC/DC's Back in Black is one of the best-selling albums of all time. All rock, no love songs or ballads or shit like that. Rising from the ashes of the sudden death of their singer, Bon Scott, the Young brothers partnered with Robert John "Mutt" Lange to produce a rock masterpiece.

Imagine that your father quickly spoke the previous paragraph to you in an overly excited voice – how would you react? Exactly as my daughter did, she shut down immediately. She never mentioned that again, she didn't want to be associated with me. Her taste in music has become darker in her teenage years – she loves thrash metal (all screaming, no melody) and she rather enjoys that other people (i.e., her parents) don't understand her and her music. OMG she sounds exactly like me when I couldn't get my mother to understand the movie "The Breakfast Club" and how teenagers are full of angst and life was just so difficult!

At home, the first great compromise between my husband and me involved music. Quite simply, he can't be in the room with any music that has a guitar or beat, nearly everything in the Leahy family collection gets on his nerves. But like a gift from the heavens, we found a solution…YACHT ROCK. Originally known as the West Coast sound, it's soft rock from the late 1970s/early 1980s that combines smooth soul, smooth jazz, R&B, funk, and disco. Our Amazon Prime station plays the same artists over and over again. That might sound annoying but it's exactly the artists of my childhood: Steely Dan, Boz Scaggs, the Doobie Brothers, Toto, Michael McDonald, Carly Simon, Bill Withers, Kenny Loggins and George Benson. It's a perfect mix that works around the house or lounging around in the pool.

Chapter Seventeen

July 2015 - Marriage Equality and My Fur Baby

We never had any pets growing up – my father hated animals and since our house was already littered with children and noise, I'm pretty sure that a family pet would have only added to the stress and animosity between my parents. My husband is a dog person and has had one or more of them at a time for over twenty-five years. He prefers girl dogs and in our home, our Chihuahua Felicia speaks to us daily. When I say speak I don't mean bark. I mean that Felicia has conversations with me through my husband's falsetto voice. What's even funnier is when Felicia and my husband argue and he is voicing both sides of the discussion.

I guess we should start with the backstory (courtesy of my creative husband) of Ms. Felicia Maria McGillicuddy Owen Leahy Rockefeller. She came from Bel Air and lived in the lap of luxury. Life was wonderful with her chef, gardener and pool boy. One fateful night she went to a party and someone slipped her a Mickey – she woke up in a field in Stockton, California (330 miles away) without her cell phone or purse and couldn't get back home. She wound up in Portland, Oregon and luckily was adopted by a big bear with an even bigger heart. She has blossomed as we have spoiled her to no end. She is deliciously happy and settled with her mother (my husband) and me. Quite the ham, she owns more than enough adorable outfits, although with that "Taco Bell Spokesmodel" ensemble, she looks like she's seriously questioning her life choices.

Glowing Up Gay

The undeniable love that Felicia has for my husband is a thing of beauty. I know that she also fancies me and enjoys my company and freely sits on my lap whenever my other half is not around. When he is home Ms. Felicia is glued to him, wanting his attention and affection. She's not an active dog – she's round in the middle and doesn't like to go outside (don't tell her that I told you, I'll get in trouble!). All she wants is to touch or be adjacent to someone she loves so that she can relax and sleep. We often wonder what trauma she must have suffered before we adopted her. All we want is to take care of her and all she wants is to feel safe and protected. And isn't that all any of us desires?

For my husband, Felicia is one of many children (Mollie, Clarice, Cooper) that he has raised over the years. Any adult in this country can adopt a pet – there are hardly any restrictions, no laws banning the LGBTQ+ community from owning animals. Conversely, if he wanted to raise a child by himself or with a former partner, there would have been obstacles – many states have had laws on the books to prevent same-sex couples from adopting, and many still do. I can't truly appreciate his struggles – for nearly all of his adult life, the idea of having children wasn't automatic as it is with straight couples. If it was going to happen, it would have to be planned, he may have needed to go to court. He might have had to go to another country, and that means money. It's such an awakening when you realize that your privileges are barriers to others. What you perceive as typical and customary may be extraordinary and unreachable to others.

Marriage Equality was a watershed moment for the LGBTQ+ community, it was the culmination of the hopes and efforts of so many pioneers as they fought to have legal protections secured for the person they loved. June 26, 2015, the date of the Supreme Court decision, will never be forgotten. I hate to admit this, but it was just another Friday for me. I was divorced at the time and still in my 'not quite gay/definitely not straight' phase of my Coming Out journey. That decision didn't pack an emotional punch – I was never forced to accept a relationship that was 'almost' a marriage, like a civil union. Just like gay adoption, it's another example of how the LGBTQ+ community was not seen as real until recently – our love was not real and our ability to create a nurturing family and raise children was doubted. While I don't think that Marriage Equality will ever be negated (it's the law of the land and nearly every major US company signed amicus briefs supporting it), some members of the Supreme Court have already stated that they don't support it, that they want it overturned. We still live in a society where a judicial system is debating how to take away rights from one group while the same rights are given to another. Remember it wasn't just about Marriage, the other half of that decision was Equality. Things like adding your spouse to your health insurance, creating a will, doing taxes together, changing your last name to match your husband, being legal parents or guardians – those became automatic with that decision.

I've been married for over two years and my 'Marriage Equality moment' is how powerful the word HUSBAND is when I describe my spouse. It's wonderful and still a little weird. IMHO, it elevates him in conversations. When we were dating I would call him my boyfriend or by his first name. The same thing when we got engaged, he was my fiancé. The word husband shouldn't be a surprise – it's a logical extension of our evolved relationship. Legally we are married – I'm his husband and he is mine. But it's more than that – during a typical year at my company, I interact with around 300-400 sales and marketing professionals from around the world. To the best of my knowledge, there are maybe 2-3 other LGBTQ+ folks. There may be more, but they are not out at work, or at least not to me. I am not aware of anyone that is married to someone of the same gender. When I use that simple word to signify our legally-recognized relationship, I feel like I'm declaring that I am just like everyone else. I feel compelled to remind you that I'm not shouting this from the rooftops. I talk about my marriage just like everyone else and the most beautiful part is that I don't have to code-switch and change his name and/or gender in my conversations, it's a natural addition to any work discussion.

It's not all wine and roses —conversations where I mention my husband are almost exclusively full of women. I have plenty of male co-workers who are great friends and supportive of me and my relationship. I know them, I trust them. But I don't know everyone's background and comfort level. I can't be naïve and think that everyone will be supportive and happy for me. Some will believe that what I've done is illegal, that my love for another man is wrong. I guess I see myself as one of many who puts a face on same-sex marriage to those who don't know anyone. I am here and I am queer.

We've come a long way with Marriage Equality and gay couples on television that have an adopted child (Cam & Mitch from *Modern Family* – LOVE THEM!), but we're not all the way there yet. I work for a company that has a perfect score with the Human Rights Council, but I also lived in a state where an employer or landlord can fire you/evict you for being gay. It doesn't happen often, but it's still an option. You want to think that progress around things like same-sex marriage is linear. Unfortunately it's a jagged line of ups and downs, progresses and declines. Being 'out' at work and social media is dramatically different than it was 5-7 years ago, which is still light years ahead of where we were 20-40 years ago. My coming out journey, and eventually my marriage, was a product of my ability to be comfortable in my skin (and finding my Bear Model!) along with a general change in culture. It's like we were on parallel paths – I was slowly growing into my true self and we as a country were getting ready to be more accepting. Allowing love and fairness to win over hate and fear.

You may have heard of <u>The Five Love Languages</u>, ways that you and your partner can express and experience love. For my husband, it's Receiving Gifts and for me, it's 1,000% Physical Touch. I want to hold hands as much as possible, to be held (the little spoon) when we lay down together. I feel safe when I'm in his arms like he's protecting me – it's both physical and emotional. In some ways it feels like I'm admitting a weakness, but it's just the way I'm wired – the touch of my husband (he holding me or me touching his furry arms, chest and back) both excites me and relaxes me. I truly didn't know this about myself when I came out. That's one of the most intriguing parts of my coming out journey – I escaped from a damaging relationship and I didn't know who I was, what I wanted out of life or what made me happy. So many of the emotional epiphanies that I've experienced over the past 9+ years are cataloging things that I've learned about myself. . My ongoing effort to hide parts of me prevented me from discovering Peter; unfortunately, I self-stunted his growth for at least two decades.

Chapter Eighteen

My Late-Blooming Education and Corporate Follies

I've been in marketing for almost twenty-five years and am blessed that I've worked in a field that I love, in a career tailored to what makes me tick and gets me excited. I'm more creative than analytical – I love identifying unique strategies or combining multiple ideas to solve problems.

Just like maturing after my triplet brother and sister and coming out of the closet in my 40s, I was a late bloomer in my chosen vocation. When the triplets were in junior high school (we didn't call it middle school back in the day), our district sent us to Children's Hospital in Boston for assessments. I met Dr. Melvin Levine and he told my parents that I was special and that I should attend boarding school. In a nutshell, that's what we did – I lived away from home as a hyper and bright pre-pubescent fourteen-year-old. My parents also split up the triplets and favored one of them over the other two. I am incredibly fortunate that they invested in me – I needed to mature and establish my own identity. When I came home on the weekend, I was more polite than my brother and sister, it's only natural since I wasn't butting heads with my mother on a day-to-day basis. Unfortunately it created a 'me vs. them' mentality between us. My brother and I were joined at the hip until I went away, and you could see that he was hurt by my absence. We grew apart and never recovered – it's like my personal growth came at a cost. I developed a new identity and network of friends and lost my older brother.

Quick note on Dr. Levine, the former Chief of Ambulatory Pediatrics at Children's Hospital in Boston. He was a Rhodes Scholar and a best-selling author and made many appearances on the Oprah Winfrey show. He's no longer alive – he killed himself in 2011 when he was indicted for decades of child abuse to dozens of young boys. The day that the indictment was opened, he put a shotgun in his mouth and took his life. In preparation for the case, the Suffolk County Attorney's Office contacted my mother and me and asked if we wanted to be included in the Class Action suit. I declined, but my mother volunteered a strange encounter that I had forgotten – it freaks me out now as an adult.

During our visit, he was meeting with me and my parents and me and at one point, he massaged my groin. My mother said that I gave him a dirty look at the time, but she didn't think twice about it. When I challenged her on why she didn't say anything, she said in her thick Boston accent, "Peetah, he was a doctor. We trusted him!" Later that summer, before I attended school, I went to his home by myself to review my class schedule options – he lived on a farm with cows and lambs. I don't know if he touched me or did something inappropriate, but I am flabbergasted that my parents let their very tiny son spend time alone with a man who semi-violated him right before their eyes. I said to her, "Mom, how the hell did you let me go to his house by myself? Where's the creep factor?" I share this not to condemn my parents or to beat the already dead horse of Dr. Levine's abuses, but to show you that sometimes parents get it wrong. We can't judge people for their decisions after the fact. My parents would never have knowingly let an abuser touch me.

High school was 99% excellent for me, except for a hazing incident when I was a freshman – a sophomore targeted me and other freshmen and was kicked out. He attempted to sue the school that he was a victim of racial bias, there was a story about it in The New York Times. I was not a good student as I lacked the discipline to properly study and I didn't have parents around to keep me on track and/or push me. My academic problems continued with the SATs and the college admissions process. I was strong in Math but struggled with English and my scores reflected it. While my friends were applying to and getting into colleges like Columbia, Brown, Dartmouth and Colorado College, I applied to a couple of private colleges (Colby, Bates, Boston College) and was only accepted by the state university, the University of Massachusetts at Amherst. It shouldn't be a surprise that I ended up at UMASS, I didn't have the grades or SAT scores to meet the admission requirements from those other schools. When I graduated, I was embarrassed at the time – I felt like I was not as smart or as polished as my friends.

I'm proud to say that I used my "I'm not good enough" feelings to get my shit together and become an excellent student. It's like I figured everything out when I went to college (it probably doesn't hurt that I was now paying for part of my education). I took extra classes, didn't go out much and focused on getting almost all A's and I graduated in three years (NERD ALERT!). I achieved Phi Beta Kappa and was proud that I turned it around – I felt like I finally belonged with my high school friends. Additionally, I published a research article with a professor, "Understanding and Treating Perfectionistic College Students." From someone who graduated high school with poor writing ability and below-average standardized test scores, publishing a literature review article was a sweet turnaround.

It's probably not hard to figure out that I knew the research subject well – I was probably looking in a mirror. At the time, I wanted to be perfect; I didn't want to be different in any way. I wanted to prove that I was as smart as my friends, I wanted my father to love me, and I wanted to have a girlfriend.

My major was psychology – I was driven by a need to help people. While I did have positive intent, I was also masking my problems and insecurities while supporting others. On the outside I was a successful student, I was young with luxurious blonde hair and a pretty girlfriend. I was smart, she was smart. On the outside we looked like the perfect couple and we were truly happy, but of course it was just a mask, I was just beginning to effectively hide my shame and perfect my self-hatred.

By the time I was a senior I realized that I didn't want that career – I couldn't separate my desire to help people from my competitive nature. One of the best traits of a therapist is to be neutral, to be like water. You don't get involved, do not become emotionally invested in your clients. I couldn't do that. When I was finally in an environment with patients, I didn't like it at all.

My first job out of college was as an Architectural Reporter for a Construction News Magazine. My girlfriend and I relocated from Boston to Southern California, joining my brother and older sister. I'm fairly certain that I got the job because of my merits, but it didn't hurt that I knew someone in a photo in my future boss's office. It was the parent that lived in one of the dorms from my boarding school, 3,000 miles away. What luck! What a small world! Before hiring me my boss called his friends back east – they said that I was a bit hyper (a fair assessment) but in general a great kid. This job gave me a company car and I drove around Santa Monica, Pacific Palisades, Malibu and Westwood interviewing architects and engineers on future construction projects. Not a bad life for a 22-year-old!

SoCal didn't suit us so we only spent two years there and I transferred within my company back to New England, as my girlfriend pursued her master's degree in Social Work. Then I found my first marketing role with a family-owned architecture & construction company – they designed and built YMCAs and athletic facilities for small colleges and universities. As we say in Boston, that family was wicked smaht. They ran THREE successful businesses in one location – a design & construction company, a family-oriented ski resort in Vermont (Smuggler's Notch) and a vacation rental property in Martha's Vineyard.

After a couple of years in a junior marketing role, it was time to further my career and that meant getting my MBA. I was not going to repeat the laissez-faire effort and crappy results from the SAT, so I registered for a test prep course and took 10-12 practice exams. It worked – my score improved dramatically as I studied and I achieved a 740 on the exam (94% percentile at the time). I targeted a top-notch school (Duke University's Fuqua School of Business) and was accepted. And with my great college grades, they awarded me a scholarship that covered half of my tuition! Going to Duke was smart for me personally and professionally but leaving for North Carolina did represent the last time I ever lived in Boston. It was tough leaving my high school posse, my true friends.

Throughout my marketing career I've endured the many ups-and-downs of corporate life – each employer was a case study in horrible management and/or toxic culture:

COMPANY #1 – UNWILLING TO CHANGE: a leading manufacturer of paper-based greeting cards. The culture there was fantastic – lots of respect for the creative process and lots of gay people as I pretended not to notice. All employees are driven by personal expressions; they "get" the power of cards. I loved cards too (still do). It's the reason why they hired me, why I wanted to move to the Midwest and work for them. However, I was young and thankful for my first post-MBA marketing role and I didn't look into the leadership group – it was conservative. I'm not talking politically, I mean stuck in the past, unable to evolve as a business and risk-averse. During my time, there were dozens of companies and technologies that they could have purchased to become a bigger and more successful business. But that's not what drove them – they were singularly focused on doing one thing – creating beautiful and very profitable cards. When I was there, the profit margins for the greeting card category within grocery stores were sky high – only bagged ice was higher! The business was dying – sending paper cards did not align with younger people and the Internet was undermining their business model – it's hard to compete with free.

COMPANY #2 – CORPORATE MERGER GONE WRONG: a major orange juice company that's owned by a large food manufacturing conglomerate. My first few years with this company were magical – the business was profitable, I was the brand manager for tropical fruit blends and I was involved in all sorts of marketing efforts, including sponsoring Jeff Gordon and NASCAR; and Spanish-language advertising. Our parent company purchased another company, and we were incorporated into this new acquisition. From the start it was a mess – the cultures didn't match, go-to-market strategies didn't align and annoyingly, nearly all of my company's sales leaders were let go. It was a classic case of 'you need to do things our way, we are larger than you and successful.'

With the merger, we had a small reduction in headcount – we eliminated two marketing positions out of twenty on our team. Then I found out that marketing roles associated with my team were transferring to Chicago and I had to re-apply for my own job (NOTE: some Chicago-area marketers who were let go from the acquisition company were itching for the same roles). Surprisingly, someone from my marketing team quit soon after that and I wanted that person's position – I wanted to stay in Florida as we had just purchased a new home! I heard about the open role as I attended an offsite meeting. I came home and told my wife and she encouraged me to ask my marketing Vice President for the position. Here's the scene – we're in the bedroom holding hands, I'm standing and she's on her knees, praying that God will let us stay in our home, as our daughter was just born. I run to the office, eagerly hoping that I can convince my VP to consider me for the role. I walk into his office and before I say my first word he says, "don't worry Peter, I already recommended you for the role." Nice! That victory was short-lived, the whole marketing team was moved to Chicago within a year, but I was not offered a role there, even though that's exactly where I wanted to move – it was the ideal location to help my son recover.

COMPANY #3 – CRAPPY WORK ENVIRONMENT + CRAPPY BUSINESS RESULTS: a company that manufactured disposable aluminum baking pans. I know what you're saying, "Peter, why did you ever leave a company that makes a product that sounds so damn exciting!" First, I was thankful that they hired me and moved us to Chicago – a necessary step for my son's development. I only worked here for a year, the most miserable year of my life – everything in my personal life was a shitstorm – we bought a house that I didn't like (I actually said no and my wife overruled me), my son was getting better but it was a struggle, we made no friends and didn't enjoy the climate, my commute to work was hellish (46 miles each way) and I worked in a small office with very little day-to-day interaction with people. While the business was profitable, the majority of sales occurred in the fourth quarter – it lost money for the rest of the year. During my short time there, there was an accounting error and that fourth quarter windfall didn't happen. The parent company relies on those consistent results for their quarterly report to shareholders and when that didn't happen, the shit hit the fan. The General Manager was fired and eventually the business was sold.

COMPANY #4 – MERGERS & ACQUISITION & FUNNY MONEY: a deli products division of a turkey company. I swear I did my homework with this company – my boss was highly regarded and he was aligned with upper management. I liked my boss – creative, smart and energetic, I believe he saw the same in me and I was ready to grow roots in this company with him, I was one of 'his guys.' Within twelve months it all fell apart – the parent company decided to sell this business and they broke up the band: my boss was demoted; the Vice President survived and disowned my previous boss; and the President left. An acquisition manager came in to run the business. Maybe manage isn't the right word – he was hired to make the company look good on paper so that it could be sold. I was asked to be part of the transition team and it was the first time that I'd ever been given a bonus contract. I was offered an extra $90,000 if I stayed in my role and the company was sold within the next 12-24 months. It sounds like a big number and it was! But there was some fine print – my role was bonus eligible (I didn't receive one the year before, poor results) and now that bonus was guaranteed…and that amount was part of the bonus. Alarmingly, there was another catch. I needed to stay with the company during its sale and be employed for at least six months after the purchase. If I was let go at any point, the incremental money was forfeited.

I signed the contract and stayed with the company for another 2-3 months, but my heart wasn't in it. I had no faith that the company was going to fulfill its promise. Plus my son was improving and we were looking forward to a fresh start, in a new city. We didn't like Chicago and we wanted to leave his diagnosis behind, we didn't want him to be labeled (plus we wanted it to remain a secret). From a climate perspective, going from Florida to Chicago is a major step backward – I wanted to live somewhere warmer. Atlanta became our next home!

Chapter Nineteen

How My Marketing Career Blossomed in the Right Environment

My post-MBA marketing career did not start as smoothly and as wonderfully as I had hoped. I started in COMPANY #1's Leadership Development Program, which allowed me to join different business units for 3-4 months and learn about the company's different businesses. I started on Holiday Cards (I planned a season of Thanksgiving Cards!), worked on the Wal-Mart team, moved the collectible ornaments group and finally corporate strategy. The company was flush with money yet still decades behind in technology. How about this for contrast: I was assigned to a desk for Holiday Cards with a phone that had a red light – it was a shared phone with another intern and the phone lit up when the other person was using it! I feel like I'm dreaming – I thought Party Lines died like 50 years ago! A year later we were living large with corporate strategy – the entire team visited San Francisco and Sonoma Valley for 2-3 days as an 'inspiration and current trends' trip.

I settled in a role on Everyday Cards (think birthday, baby, wedding, anniversary, etc.) and within a year, I was told by management that I should pursue another career, that I did not have what it takes to make it in marketing. Angry and embarrassed, I looked for another company and relocated to Florida within months. I enjoyed living in Florida for nearly five years – both my children were born there – but in the end, my life was unraveling professionally (merger, marketing team consolidation, move to Chicago) and personally (my son's unknown illness, flying around the country to track down possible therapies and cures). While my son thrived in a great education system in Chicago and with his alternative medicine doctor, both of my short-term employments were problematic. Was I cursed? Would I ever find a company where I could grow as a marketing expert? I mentioned earlier that the move from Chicago was about starting anew for my son, but the same could be said for my marketing career. I had been out of business school for eight years and had worked for four employers in three different cities. I looked like a nomad – where's the long-term plan? Are you ever going to settle down and establish yourself?

We were fortunate with the move to Atlanta in May 2006 – thankfully we found a buyer for our house (we did not make any money on that property; we chose the wrong house). The housing market would soon crumble in a few months – our agent didn't sell another home that year! We found a LARGE home in Atlanta (three stories, six bedrooms, five bathrooms), but something weird happened – my introduction to the South. As the seller and I went back and forth in negotiating the price, another buyer knocked on the door and offered a full-price offer. The seller accepted this – a BIG no-no with their real estate agent. My agent and this rogue buyer got into a heated discussion because the other party claimed that "God wants me to have this house." Oh brother, a classic case of prosperity theology.

Yes our home was WAY too big for our needs and the mortgage was the most I could qualify for and we purchased at the peak of the market. We were the trifecta of stupidity! We bought a home in an established neighborhood called The Polo Fields (totally snobby). Admittedly, we were just like other families who overextended themselves: assuming that the housing market would always appreciate; that a home is the safest financial investment. When we did file for bankruptcy in 2010 we kept the home, but then short-sold it in 2014 during the divorce.

I started with my company in May 2006 and there was drama from the start. I thought I had landed in a perfect spot as they were looking for external applicants with MBAs and previous marketing experience to build their marketing talent. All previous marketing "hires" were existing sales professionals that wanted corporate experience. The previous marketer had reported directly to the hard-nosed salesperson but when I came in, I reported to the marketing director. Well guess what, these guys hated each other, they refused to communicate directly with each other: I felt like the child of parents who hated each other, I know how that feels! My salesperson and I did not get along – we both had clear ideas of what marketing meant to our customers. Although he was retiring within the next few months, he reached out to his director after I was on the job for only three weeks and said, "get rid of Peter, he's not going to work out."
Another Business Development Manager replaced Mr. Hard-Nose and we worked together for only 30 days. Why so short? It might have something to do with him cheating on his wife (a recovering cancer survivor) with a secretary from one of our customers. My company

found out and fired him immediately. Stuff goes on in every company and we're no different, it's just that all this shit occurred back-to-back. When I reflect on the most wonderful times within my company, my British boss (who later became the North American President) evokes many wonderful & funny memories:

    a. MEETING RICHARD PETTY – I leveraged some contacts from my NASCAR marketing days to get Pit Passes for the Atlanta Motor Speedway and we are introduced to The King! As we approach him, my boss loudly announces that he will say, "loved you in the Cars movie!" I was mortified and I shouted back, "DO NOT embarrass me in front of Richard Petty," like he even knows who the hell I am.

    b. DAMAGING MY CAR – As we're heading to the racetrack, my boss mistakenly hits my car while backing out of his driveway. I tell him that it's no big deal, my car was rather beat up already. I didn't tell any co-workers, hoping that keeping this secret would endear me to him. Little did I know that he was such a charmer, he brazenly tells the story of cracking up my car and I'm the one who gets embarrassed by it.

    c. STOCK OPTION GIFT – One year my company did not meet its financial results and there were no year-end bonuses. My team over delivered on our results and my boss petitioned for me to receive a one-time gift of stock options – OMG, so thoughtful and generous! Why is this important? These became vested years later and I was able to afford a lawyer to leave my wife.

    d. LONDON OLYMPIC GAMES – one of my co-workers swam in the 1976 Olympics for her home country, Columbia. Her daughter followed in her footsteps and qualified for the 2012 games in London. My co-worker (the gorgeous lady in the photo, chapter thirteen) is a talented sales leader and the boss asked if she would go to England to "train" that team during that summer. I'm just beaming with love and admiration for this man - there is nothing more precious than your company enabling you to see your child compete on the world's stage?

    e. SWEETNESS 101- During Pride Month (it's June, BTW), my coming out story was featured in a trade magazine. His note to me when it came out: "*Peter this is amazing and thoroughly deserved recognition for you. I do not think you realize what an inspiration you are to everyone around you both professionally and personally. The courage you showed in "coming out" and the day-to-day involvement in PRIDE and across the Employee Resource Groups has clearly made us a more inclusive place. You should be thoroughly pleased with yourself for all you have done to advance Inclusion, Caring, and Authenticity."*

f. BITING HUMOR – After my son received a four-year college scholarship from my company, I saw my boss at an after-work Happy Hour and he shared his cheeky humor: "Peter, you know that your son gets to keep the scholarship even if we sack you."

g. MY ENGAGEMENT PARTY – My co-workers celebrated our engagement and my boss gladly accepted the invitation. He's naturally a jolly and personable chap but he made me feel so special that night, like I was his son, that my happiness was as important to him as it was to me.

He's a great leader, a wonderful man and a special friend. He's retired now and I love that I have all of these memories, that I'm one of many people that can testify to his magnanimous personality and generous spirit. Our company is driven by its culture and the behaviors of our senior leaders and the impact that he's had on me is his legacy.

I specifically chose the word Legacy because that's how I think about my marketing career – what potential impact did I have on my company, professionally and personally? I will remind the Dear Reader (Stephen King reference) that I am not a doctor or teacher or anyone else who can have a significant impact on the health and well-being of others. I am a creative problem solver and 'Ideas Machine' (my self-described moniker on LinkedIn) who has found his passion in helping drive consumer products into the hands of consumers and businesses. As a bonus I know WAY too many details on the features & benefits and manufacturing processes associated with greeting cards, orange juice, deli meat and toilet paper.

I'm at an age where I can look back with both happiness and sadness: have I made an impact with a particular team or project? What consumer products or marketing programs can I say that I launched or supported? You can easily point to things that you helped create, but the human side is more powerful and harder to quantify. Did I live an inspired life? Have I made a difference in the lives of the people closest to me? How will I be remembered? Does my perception of me align with how others see me? All of these things are important to me but admittedly, most of my marketing career occurred through the lens of the old Peter: I was happy when I was working but you've seen some of the struggles and inner demons that I was fighting. I wasn't the fully realized version of me. With the fully unleashed rainbow Peter, I'm working on growing myself as a marketing guru and continuous learner!

I am lucky to have had angels who helped me develop into the man that I was meant to be and that's the beauty of finally figuring out who you are and where you belong. I am happy with myself 24/7 and have what I need to live a fulfilled life with my husband. Material things are great (I will never turn down the opportunity to purchase matching outfits with my bear model), but it's time and memories that fuel my passion. It's supporting my family, friends and co-workers and helping them figure things out for themselves. The qualities that I hope other people see in me are:

1. HONESTY / TRUSTWORTHINESS – you might find this ironic, coming from a man who hid his identity for most of his adult life. Hear me out! I have seen the light; I am a reformed

liar. I don't pretend to be something that I'm not and have no interest in trying to impress people. I lived that life: I hated myself, it jaded how I saw people and my ability to make connections and truly help or impact others. If you like me, I'm thrilled and if you don't, then that's cool. I'm not everyone's cup of tea. I appreciate it when my friends and associates are real with me: you don't have to pretend; I'm not going to judge you. Over several chapters you've seen that I lived a flawed life and made myself miserable; I was afraid all the time. I'm never going back to that way of thinking and I'll do everything in my power to do the same for the ones I love.

2. FUN/HAPPY/GOOFY – I've always loved dry humor and Dad Jokes – it aligns with my sometimes-twisted thinking (creativity and madness are kissing cousins!). I've always enjoyed my ability to laugh at myself (male pattern baldness in your 20s will do PLENTY of damage to the fragile male ego) and now I can look back at the old Peter and see a mixed bag of agony and ecstasy. I laugh because I'm thriving with an exuberant authentic life since coming out of the closet; whereas I struggled for decades to fit into the wrong alternative lifestyle. My happy-go-lucky nature was clearly articulated in a recent personality test. I am a STRONG "Sunshine Yellow" which has the primary characteristics of being sociable, dynamic, demonstrative, enthusiastic and persuasive. Every personality type has pros and cons; my style is slow to give up and eager to try new ideas. But the same passion that drives me and others like me can hurt you when you have trouble with criticism and you take work-related failures personally.

3. HOPEFULLY I MADE YOUR LIFE BETTER – this isn't a conscious set of activities or goals for myself, it's more like a state of mind. I know I'm reminding you for the 87th time, but I am not a Zen master; I have not achieved a higher level of consciousness. However, I do know what makes me tick: I am a pleaser, I receive some form of self-fulfillment in helping others, and I recognize the strengths and pitfalls associated with that drive to make others happy. It used to be that when I helped

create a moment of happiness or levity, I fed off of it. I needed that to make me feel better about myself and conveniently, I was masking my internal suffering. Now that I have my own inner light (Dad Joke - it's totally Sunshine Yellow), that's the part of me that drives all of my senses. When you breathe light and feel love, that's what you see in the people that you love and it's also how you hear them. Similarly, it forms the words that you say from your heart and most importantly to me, it drives the desire to make a physical connection with you. Ideally that connection is a big ole bear hug, but a high five or pat on the back works just fine in a pinch.

Over the years I've completed some leadership training classes – here are some 2018 highlights, starting with the Top 5 things that I rated about myself:

To be fair, I also rated myself as average or poor on things like "I have a range of sponsors to support my career development" and "I effectively work with my mentors to facilitate and achieve goals." Just another example of I am a work in progress and that after many years of being stuck and hiding who I was, I am well on my evolution journey to make an impact personally and professionally. That's my Legacy – I will make a difference in my company in Marketing and Diversity & Inclusion and hopefully both. My company supported me during dark times and helped me blossom. I'd love to return the favor.

Chapter Twenty

If At First You Don't Succeed…

So apparently I'm a Late Bloomer. For many of my significant milestones-events, the first takes didn't work out and I would usually find success on the rebound. Being late started early for me (can't stop me with the Dad Jokes). My brother and sister went through puberty about 18 months ahead of me – yes, during high school I looked like their younger brother (I was a tiny kid to begin with). I have a picture but I WON'T be sharing that one. As you can see from the photo of us from Chapter Thirteen, I'm now the tallest! My life is full of experiences where I learned to be resilient and to persevere.

Take One	Take Two
The baby that did not go to term	Finally becoming parents – boy and girl
Poor high school grades and SAT scores, not accepted to the school of my choosing	Fantastic GMAT score, excellent college grades, attending a top-tier business school
Marriage #1 – living through fear, abuse, struggling to be straight	Marriage #2 – living through love, normal, proudly out of the closet
Working for numerous companies – not finding the role and culture that worked for me	Helping create the culture and blossoming my marketing talents in the right environment

Some of these items may seem trivial; you could argue that I don't know what it's like to really struggle. That last part is a fair point – I recognize that I'm a white male and many doors and opportunities will always be available based on my appearance; I don't need to fight for equality like women and/or people of color. As I've become more aware (aka, getting older, which means I don't put up with other people's bull), I have an even greater appreciation for people that have overcome any form of hardship or handicap (physical, financial, etc.). I'm inspired by those who decide that they want something different – they want a better life or they want to change the life that they have.

But Peter, didn't you just type almost 50,000 words to do just that? You've shared story after story of things that you've endured, aren't you inspirational? Didn't you effectively re-engineer your life and start over? Of course I did. I'm proud of what I've accomplished in a relatively short time. Obviously I'm in a good place and happy with the many changes in my life, but I struggle with giving myself any credit. I created an imperfect life and attempted to make it work: an illusion of happiness and success for which I paid the price for living that lie. I won't get those years back, I have no one to blame but myself for my struggles.

But overcome I did. I should be thanking my parents, as each of them instilled in me what they did best (mom – the consistent caretaker, dad – the reliable provider) while they made themselves and their marriage secondary, focusing on the children.

It might be a strange way to think about it, but for the most part, I have initially failed at nearly everything I have ever tried. Except for accumulating and spitting out random facts and trivia – that God-given talent is wired in me from head to toe! Seriously, I am a product of eventually finding my groove and my place in this world. Now that I think about it, I shouldn't portray being a late bloomer or succeeding on the second go-round as a bad thing. So what if your first relationship, job, or career didn't work out? The whole point of this autobiographical digest is to keep trying, to keep striving for the things that make you happy. And if I can do it, there's no reason why you can't follow in my unconventional footsteps. I didn't set out to share my story to pound my chest and proclaim my steely resolve and unshakeable will. I did it because I wanted to help others – ideally it would inspire you to think about your current life choices and make changes if they're not the real you or at least not the life that you imagined.

Chapter Twenty-One

August 2020 - Building a Life with the Bear of My Dreams

This modern-day love story has humble beginnings – we were friends on Facebook, living 2,598 miles apart. We were 'friends' but truly didn't know each other, didn't have any connection or DMs, nothing much beyond liking each other's posts. What I didn't know at the time was that someone had a little crush on me. He saw my sunny personality and knew I was an active father; not having any children of his own may be one of his greatest regrets. Now I share his disappointment with the way that my relationship with my children has devolved. They're missing out on a tremendous step-father and my husband is missing the chance to influence and guide and love two young adults as they embark on their post-education life.

Everyone has their story about how they met and how the relationship came to be, and we are no different. My husband lived outside of Portland, Oregon at the time and he saw one of my Facebook posts, I was in Portland. He was surprised and rather disappointed that I didn't reach out to him directly to meet in person and maybe have a drink. The reason why I didn't was that I was in Portland, Maine.

We had a chuckle but that's all we needed to start creating a connection. Nothing happened that day or that week but within a few weeks, I reached out to him again and said the two words that forever changed our lives: "hey handsome!" I was just saying hello and hoping to start a conversation. My future husband was shocked – he wasn't sure at the time if I found him attractive or if I even knew who he was. When I messaged him, he was driving to Seattle to visit his best friend Ed and he asked if he could call me later. Thank goodness for both of us he did! We did the normal things to get to know each other – texting, calling, FaceTiming and then figuring out how to meet IRL.

> Side Note: I didn't know at the time that I was going to fall in love with the man of my dreams and find the one that I wanted to spend the rest of my life with, but I was definitely in the mood for a change. I was semi-dating another guy at the time long distance and it wasn't

working out. We lived over 1,000 miles apart and only saw each other every 4-6 weeks. I enjoyed his company and liked many things about him but there was one habit of his that he couldn't shake – he was always on his phone when we were together. The fact that he was glued to his phone and responding to messages from other guys was a consistent reminder that I wasn't as important to him, that being in the moment with me somehow didn't take precedent. My anger and resentment reached a boiling point during my cousin's wedding on Cape Cod. It was a gorgeous summer day and we dressed up and we spent the afternoon with my three sisters and at some point, I saw his phone light up with a message from one of those gay dating apps. It sent me over the edge that his phone was a constant third in our relationship. That wedding was the last time we saw each other. It was my Caribbean cruise all over again – I wasn't going to be anyone's backup choice. I wanted to find someone who would love me and would be fulfilled by me and me alone.

Back to the love story – we talked and FaceTimed and did all of the things that burgeoning couples do – tell your story, listen attentively to your new crush and try to look inside and see yourself with this person – do you share the same values, do you have similar interests, are you compatible sexually. It's a little bit of a checklist/job interview, but you want to make sure that you're making a smart investment. Is this a person that I can see myself with on a typical Tuesday night? Can we make dinner and watch Jeopardy together? Will he go to antique stores and estate sales? (that's a BIG YES) Will he watch sports with me, especially my Boston teams? (unfortunately a BIG NO, he hates sports). Despite that one character flaw, it was looking quite promising with this guy. He was single and wanted a serious relationship. The good news was that I was traveling to Las Vegas in a few weeks and would he be opposed to flying across the country to meet me, would he consider a short plane ride to Sin City? Pretty please?

He made the trip and it was the first of many cross-country visits of me to Portland and he to Atlanta. Our Las Vegas time was punctuated with two unforgettable moments – we saw the Beatles LOVE show from Cirque Du Soleil® and we spent a night watching the fountains and listening to classical music at The Bellagio Hotel. The LOVE show exceeded my expectations and I was already super pumped about attending . It's perfect that the first day we met, September 10, 2017, is punctuated by that experience. We ended the night at the Fountains at Bellagio – it's quite romantic –a warm night with a gentle breeze from the water and the festive atmosphere made the night seem endless. My other half used Julia Roberts's "Pretty Woman" quote and it perfectly framed our time together, "In case I forget to tell you later, I had a really good time tonight."

> Tomorrow I'm gonna see that teddy bear that I always dreamed about!!!

Tomorrow I'm gonna meet the man that I'm gonna marry 🧡🧸

> Be my protector bear and I'll make you happy every single day.

You'll be mine 😘 and I'll be yours!!!

Is it tomorrow yet? Longest 24 hours ever

Yes this is the final text that we sent each other before we met for the first time. Yes it's goofy and yes I totally love it.

He was smart when we first were getting to know each other. He stressed that our time together should be spent doing normal things, like grocery shopping or buying a new couch for me because mine was broken and he was sick of both of us falling into its low point and me smothering him / not giving him any space. He said that we shouldn't be 'vacation boyfriends.' When someone is visiting, it's easy to fill up your schedule with thing like local attractions and sample the finest restaurants, to impress them a little. When I was in Portland, he made sure that we did regular things together like cooking dinner and walking the dogs; even little things like finding out how I liked my coffee in the morning, drinking it together outside and creating tiny memories together.

The next stage in our relationship is a running joke in our household. I confidently state that I was hooked after we meet in Las Vegas; I knew I found a great guy and I was all in with taking this relationship forward. My other half claims that he was 'pretty sure' it was going to work with this Atlanta guy. You know what I'm thinking, "OK Boomer, whatever you need to make yourself feel superior."

The relationship progressed naturally – we took trips together (he showed me the Oregon Coast, his favorite place on the planet, and we met each other's circle of friends), and by Christmas 2018, it was time to meet our families. We started with his – I was the FIRST man that my husband had brought home in his 40+ years. More importantly, he hadn't been home for Christmas in 16 years. Yes this was a big deal! I may have been a little nervous about making a great first impression with the extended family but he was terrified (half joking / half serious) that I would see the cast of characters in his immediate and extended family and run for the hills. That I wouldn't consider marrying him because of all of their craziness.

Everything he shared with me about his family was true – his grandfather is the sweetest man on the planet while his grandmother was (and still is) the grumpy one. He was raised primarily by his grandparents (long story, not here) and meeting them was an opportunity to better understand the man that I was in love with and hope to marry someday. His life was stressful growing up, much more difficult than anything I had to endure. To put it mildly, he was constantly told that he was a burden and more or less he wouldn't amount to much. My heart breaks as I'm typing this. I think about the sweet and sensitive man that he is now and I shudder to think of him not receiving the emotional support and nurturing that he needed. There's even more drama and tragedy in his young life but that's his story to tell.

You may have wondered if I passed the test with his family – of course I did, I'm charming AND adorable AND funny. Have you not been digesting these pertinent facts? Joking aside, the test wasn't for me, it was for them. When I see the type of people that shaped him, it made me love him even more. I wanted to love him in the ways that his family didn't, his family couldn't. I wanted us to model a happy, stable and loving relationship. For me because I needed it and for him because he deserved it.

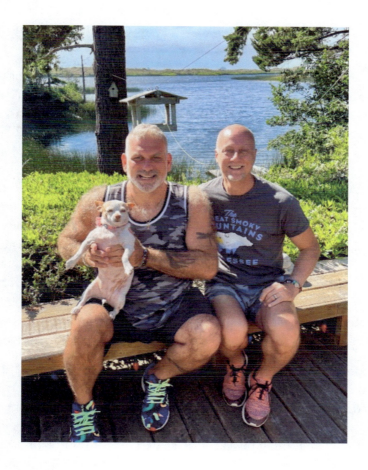

We came home to Atlanta and were casually looking at houses – ideally a Mid-Century Modern design that's close to the city. The location was important to me – I wanted to escape the suburbs, with its emphasis on religion and the limited number of gay people. The life I lived there was full of pain and littered with lies and I was slowly reinventing myself – of course I wanted to start fresh and live among LQBTQ+ families and straight allies. There was nothing available in our ideal neighborhood and we eventually drive around to our future neighborhood and we saw a blonde brick ranch that was For Sale By Owner with a shipping pod in the driveway. Nobody was home so we opened the gate to the backyard and encountered a gorgeous in-ground pool. Suddenly my husband announces, "this is it – we're buying the place." I am adamant that I'm not purchasing a home without going inside and he said, "I will design us a beautiful home." Fast forward to 60 days later, he was annoyingly correct. It was a home full of love and furniture and antiques, not modern but comfortable – it represented us.

Life is never easy all the time, never perfect, and not always what you have planned. The truth is that we didn't get this house at first. It had been for sale for two months with little-to-no interest and when we finally submitted an offer, someone else made an offer about 12 hours before us. We later found out that our real estate agent (who we later fired) was lazy or incompetent and didn't effectively represent us. One example: we asked him to submit a backup offer and he was told that the buyer wouldn't accept it. Once we switched to a more talented and aggressive agent, she secured our back-up and lo and behold, the buyer chose us! Of course I was overjoyed when I got the stupendous news but the real joy, my forever memory, is calling my husband with the great news. I cried when I could hear the shock in his voice. It was almost like the universe was working in our favor, allowing us to make memories and create traditions. Sharing that moment with him meant that we were starting our life together. It was the beginning of a beautiful relationship.

Just before we closed on the house it was Valentine's Day and I asked my husband to marry me. I shared the news on Facebook and received an unprecedented amount of love, support and well wishes from friends. That was the first time that I shared our relationship status on social media. I may be fooling myself – we shared lots of photos of us, but it felt different to announce that I was going to marry another man. That I was really, _really_ gay. My friends were happy for us, plain and simple. 99% of them didn't know the complete story that you've read. The fact that my straight and gay friends celebrated us equally felt wonderful, and maybe a little weird. Maybe 'foreign' is a better term – I was still configuring my dual identities – I had straight people/co-workers and I had my gay friends. The two groups did not know each other and I presented myself differently to each of them. But it didn't matter – I was worried that my gay friends would someone scare my straight friends with suggestive comments, but of course I was wrong. I should have seen it from another point of view. I was manufacturing drama (I'd been doing it for years!) and people just saw two guys in love who were ready to take the next step in their relationship. Finding someone to settle down with in your 40s is not that common, especially in a long-distance relationship. And whether it was luck, timing or some cosmic force, it worked out for us.

Chapter Twenty-Two

My Continuing Metamorphosis; Waiting for My Children to Come Home

With the journey that I'm on, I feel like I'm reinventing myself around every year and a half. It's not a plan, I'm not setting any specific goals, it's just happening. My first three Coming Out 18-month cycles feel like Scared, Baby Gay to Comfortable, Confident Gay to (hopefully not jaded) Older Gay. It's funny how I'm both young and old – I guess I'll always be that. You see my bald head and crow's feet around my gorgeous blue eyes, but I'll forever be young and goofy. I joked before about being jaded – it's a common affliction for gay guys my age – they've suffered through numerous struggles and bad relationships. I've lived and learned in my short time, but luckily found my life partner pretty quickly. The gay world didn't let me down like everyone did in the straight world.

Let's not forget that the sheer joy and freedom and confidence that permeate my personality are a product of the hopelessness and despair that I endured for years. It's like jumping on a trampoline – the more pressure you apply, the higher you leap! Allowing myself to be happy and deserve love and respect was my first step toward mental and physical health. I say this all the time – I don't regret my life choices. I made decisions that I thought were correct at the time and I try not to dwell on the past. Do I wish I had come out earlier in life? Of course I do – it's only natural that I would want to feel better about myself and be around my people for love and support. I used to have beautiful hair and I was naturally skinny for decades – I would have rocked tiny bathing suits for years! The point is that I did change, I finally told myself that it doesn't need to be this way – I didn't need to remain in an abusive relationship that was going nowhere. I guess you could say I went from 'STOP' to 'START.' I had nearly given up on life and had stopped believing in myself. I was frozen with fear, afraid to see if there were people like me, if there was a place to belong. And I didn't listen to my fucking gut! That was the icing on the cake (ironic of course, I couldn't enjoy cake anymore). At the time I didn't listen to my body – it was telling me that my toxic relationship was harmful to my health. From an emotional perspective, I almost have a tiny bit of sympathy for my ex-wife. Everything that I've shared about her is true and there's even crazier shit that's not fit to print, but I was slowly dying on the inside – I'm sure that I walked around all day with a rain cloud over my head. I must have been a miserable partner for many years – nothing in my life at the time made me truly happy. On page one I shared that I don't know why I was in the closet for 40 years and in the same way, I'll never truly understand what changed inside of me that started me on my path to true happiness.

My relationship with her is winding down – alimony and child support are now complete but I am mentally prepared that she will attempt to extract more money from me. She's already taken me to court and used our children as tools of guilt to shame me into believing that I am cheap. I know that raising children is expensive but I gave her over $280,000 within an eight-year-period. I DO NOT lose any sleep because I have not provided enough financial support for my children.

I honestly went into my first marriage with the best of intentions – she will curse my name if she ever reads this. It's painfully obvious that she still hates me and blames me for ruining her life and believing that I disadvantaged our (her) children forever. If I didn't leave her when I did, I shudder to think of where I would be now. Based on the limited interactions that we still have (all text and we only chat about money and medical bills), the same issues and problems would exist. We would spend what monies we had, and most certainly money we didn't have, for our children. Sounds about right for working families – you love them and of course you want what's best for them. But it's not right if you manufacture an unsustainable environment to create one appearance while living without love on a day-to-day basis. Not only are you pretending to be one thing to outsiders, but you double the negativity by promoting a perpetually unhappy home life. It's Bad Parenting 101.

I don't know what her life looks like without the nearly $3,000 from me every month – that's not my responsibility. She is not part of my life and I don't waste energy thinking about her. I hope that she can find peace and happiness in her life, but our time is done. I would have <u>loved</u> having a relationship with her and the children and if she wasn't hell-bent on her animosity toward me, she would have loved my husband. He loves to shop! He likes pedicures! He would have enjoyed helping her with a makeover (honey, she needs it – hair AND clothing) and it probably would have been fun for both of them to take jabs at me (old wife vs. new wife). We could have been an extended family and shared holidays together – we would have loved to have the kids stay with us during the summer and live in our pool. She could have enjoyed a much-deserved break – no school AND no children. Isn't that the ultimate fantasy for every teacher that's also a parent? But no, that didn't happen and I can't get those years back with my children. She assigns all of the blame to me and is living the life that she created. She has full control and responsibility for her children and for many years received a healthy monthly dividend from her homo ex-husband.

It's no secret, I would love to have the children in my life – I will welcome them with open arms if and when they reach out with open (or at least curious) minds. I have so much to share with them and I want my husband and me to be an active part of their lives. WHEN that does happen (thinking positive!) I will be cautious at first – I won't truly know if their intentions are true or whether they are spying or digging up dirt for my ex-wife. I feel horrible for writing this down – am I saying that I don't trust my children? I guess when you are constantly lying and providing me with misinformation, you have to re-earn my trust. I'm not asking my children to choose me over their mother – I want them to know that the relationship that I had with their mother was good and bad, that we were both unhappy and living a lie and staying together for our children. I truly pray that they can realize that their mother's stories are all one-sided. I also hope that it happens soon – I'm not getting any younger!!

My transformation was a change in my philosophy and how I see the world. For many years it was about fear, shame and embarrassment – I truly believed that I 'owned' all of the bad luck and essentially, I was allowing others to be happy and live better lives (yes I know that sounds like crazy talk, I never said I was healthy back then). But now it's about love, giving and sharing. When you are truly happy with yourself you want to share that with friends and family. You are open to making your circle bigger. That's a gift that my chosen family has given to me and I want to share it with my children. I still have love in my heart for them and I can't wait to be a part of their lives again. I can't force them to come to me – it has to be their choice. Metaphorically, I'm leaving the front porch light on for them to know that there is always someone home to greet them. I'm sure it will be shocking and overwhelming to them – a home they have never entered with a step-parent that they have never met.

PROUD moment

Peter Leahy | **August 2018**

I joined K-C in 2006 and for many of my early years I was not bringing my authentic self to work. I was unhappy in my personal life and more importantly, I was hiding a big secret. I was gay and was terrified of people finding out about me – about being exposed. When you live in the closet for so many years, you build walls of defenses – you scare yourself into inaction. You fear that you will lose everything and everyone in your life will abandon you if your true identity is revealed.

In early 2013 I finally got the courage to come to terms with my sexual orientation, to no longer be embarrassed. There was not a particular event or milestone that triggered this, I guess I decided that I was not going to be afraid anymore. So, after 20+ years of marriage and two children, I decided to be true to myself and come out to my friends and family. I got a divorce and reinvented myself in my 40's. My divorce was rather ugly – my ex-wife and I went to court TWICE.

After years of suffering in silence and feeling so alone, I put myself out there via local resources (PFLAG, Gay Fathers support group, Atlanta PRIDE Festival) and found out that there were other gay dads, other 'late bloomers' like me. With their support and my new extended LGBT family, I became more confident in my identity and more comfortable in my skin. Essentially, my gay dad friends are my 'chosen family' – we learn and support each other's coming out stories and more importantly, celebrate the highs and lows of having children.

Aidan & Fiona, My Pride & Joy

Thankfully, I have been able to embrace my identity while maintaining my passion as a father. From taking my daughter to cello lessons to attending my son's academic bowl tournaments, I support their passions as I hopefully demonstrate the importance of authenticity and making yourself happy. I'll always be their goofy, Boston sports-loving dad.

My Kimberly-Clark support network (PRIDE ERG, mentor, HR) helped me tremendously along the way. Whether it was listening while I embarked on a path to discovery, or celebrating my joy & embracing my happiness, my K-C friends helped me learn to love myself. Both physically and mentally, I am happier and healthier than I was 10 years ago.

Being able to bring my whole self to work has made me a better K-Cer! I started this journey five years ago and NEVER thought I could be this happy. It's great to be actively involved in PRIDE@K-C, to proudly represent Kimberly-Clark and to connect with straight allies that support our mission. When people ask me if I work for a good company, I can honestly say that Kimberly-Clark has brought out the best in me.

My life is far from perfect, my journey is ongoing – I do not have any contact with my ex-wife and my relationship with my teenage children can be best described as 'Don't Ask, Don't Tell.' But I wouldn't change a thing – I wanted to be a father and I wanted to be true to myself, it just took me a while to achieve this. When you consider that I thought my life was pretty much over five years ago, I am immensely grateful for my friends that helped me get to where I am today.

December 2012 vs March 2018 — The New Me!

Chapter Twenty-Three

Admitting When You Need Help and Asking For It

Did you know that there's a National Coming Out Day? It's October 11th and that day was chosen because it's the anniversary of the 1987 National March on Washington for Lesbian and Gay Rights. That day is forever seared in my memory – in 2015 that was the day I marched in my first Pride parade with the Gay Fathers of Atlanta and unfortunately, my mom also died that day. I was lucky to be surrounded by so much love and joy from all of the parade supporters. Their love and acceptance were the virtual hug that I needed that day.

I am where I am today because of people, resources and support groups that gave me the tools to chart my path. For all of the times that I felt insecure or embarrassed about who I was, one of my biggest stumbling blocks was that I was alone. For many years I was afraid to reach out to others and when I finally did, you know that it worked out for me.

If you are struggling with your sexual orientation or gender identity, please know that you don't have to do this by yourself. Here's just a sampling of resources:

-ACLU: Know Your Rights: A Guide For Trans And Gender Nonconforming Students

-Berkley Gender Equity Resource Center: Coming Out

-Bisexual Resource Center: Coming Out As Bi

-Gender Expansion Project: Coming Out Resources

-Gender Spectrum: Support For Transgender Youth

-Human Rights Campaign: Resource Guide To Coming Out

-Human Rights Campaign: Coming Out Issues For Latinos And Latinas

-Human Rights Campaign: Coming Out Issues For Asian Pacific Americans

-Human Rights Campaign: Coming Out Issues For African Americans

-Human Rights Campaign: Coming Out At Work

-Human Rights Campaign: Coming Out To Your Doctor

-LGBT Youth: A Coming Out Guide For Trans Young People

-National Center For Transgender Equality: Transgender Terminology

-Ohio University LGBT Center: Coming Out As Trans*

-The Washington Post: Coming Out As Transgender And Christian

-PFLAG: Support For Transgender People And Their Families

-PFLAG: Support For Family And Friends Of LGBT Individuals

-PFLAG: Support For Straight Spouses

-PFLAG: Guide To Being A Straight Ally

-Trevor Lifeline: The Trevor Project's 24/7 LGBT Crisis And Suicide Prevention Hotline

I went to therapy for several years when I first came out of the closet – it worked for me to have an advocate that listened as I needed to de-program my negative thoughts and objectively review my previously unhealthy relationship. One of the therapeutic techniques is to write a letter but don't send it – this is all about getting your emotions on paper. Well, I did this for my father and my ex-wife, they're both in the appendix. They are raw and emotive – for both of them, I'm having a conversation that I've always wanted to have. I'm finally challenging my ex-wife and trying to understand my father. These have never been sent, so these arguments never happened and these questions have never been answered. But that's okay. You can't have a real conversation with someone who's been gone for almost twenty years (my dad) and with someone resistant to self-reflection (my ex-wife). The point is that I have made peace with both of those relationships in the past. They don't define who I am now or where I am going: onward and upward, like a rainbow unicorn.

Peter Leahy

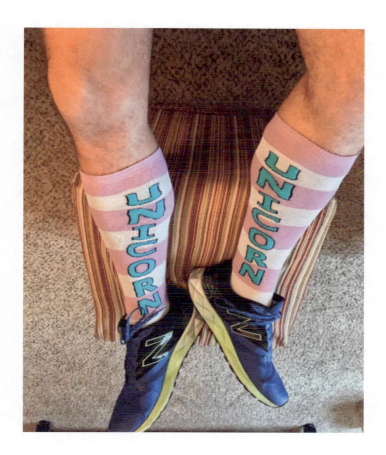

APPENDIX A – *MY EX-WIFE'S LETTER THAT WAS NEVER SENT*

One of my therapists recommended that I write a letter to my ex-wife but not send it. Here's a picture of where I was in 2016:

So it's been three years since I walked out of the door, more than two years since our divorce was final. Let's talk about what's still going on here, what's unresolved, unsettled and unsaid. I wanna get this out, review the past, present and future and MOVE ON from here. Life is too short to be reliving the past, rehashing old stories and be stuck in the same place. For the sake of the health and happiness of our children, I hope that we will eventually get to a place where we can discuss the children in productive/constructive ways while living our own separate lives.

Starting with the obvious – yes I lied to you about being gay. It's not as simple as 'when did I know.' I really chose to not believe it for years and decided to live a straight identity with my wife, who I married and was in love with for many years. The love that I felt for you at one time was real – I was happy, satisfied, trusted you and obviously we had a lot in common. I know it's hard to explain but for many years my 'gayness' was just something that stayed in the background. The two sides to that story is that I chose you because I was in love with you, but I was also super afraid of being gay. I don't know why it frightened me.

Was it fair for me to do this to you? No. Will I have to live with that for the rest of my life? Yes. Was I a perfect husband and father? No. Did you get the best version of me for over 18 years of marriage / 25 years together? Yes. I was all in with the marriage and being the father to our children. I love being a dad, I WANTED to be a dad. I felt like it was my calling. Was it ideal the way that our marriage ended? No. I wish that it could have been different. But we can't change the past, we need to move on.

As we review the last 10 years of marriage, I see two things – the first is banding together to focus on our son's recovery. It's a fucking miracle that we recovered him. And yes, you get most of the credit for his improvement. I can never say thank you enough for helping him become the young man that he is now. You were just what our son needed. I do have one beef – during our divorce negotiation, you said "remember, I'm the one that saved him." That hurt A LOT. That's the worst thing that you have ever said to me. It's so selfish – I will never forgive you for it. You are not a god – you're a passionate mother. And remember that they are <u>our</u> children, not yours.

The second thing is our separation — the twisted morphing of our relationship. We were sick, we were wrong. We were not modeling a successful relationship and not doing right by the children. Now I can play pop psychologist and tell you what happened to you. At some point you decided "I've had a shitty life, I now want what I want, I <u>deserve</u> what I want."

You bought the house to complete with that woman that we knew in Florida. You OVER-decorated your classroom (with furniture from our house!) to overcompensate for your insecurities as a teacher. I feel like almost all of your decisions are based on creating an appearance — your car, your classroom, the children's fashionable clothes. You spend money to buy love, to buy respectability. I'm not sure what you're hiding or running from, but what you are doing is wrong. You equate money with love. There are no bonus points for spending / running out of money. You cannot use 'for the children' as an excuse for everything. You are not a fucking adult. Grow. Up. Now. You're hurting yourself and the children. I'm going to be preachy here, but your role as a mother is to prepare the children for adulthood. When is that gonna start? They don't value money; they don't do anything — they have no responsibilities. Do you really think this is working? What's it gonna take for you to realize that you're doing a disservice to our children? I can't help you see it, but I pray that you realize it sooner versus later.

I am gay. All of my friends are gay. I will have a boyfriend someday and hopefully I'll have a husband. This will happen — you can't stop it, wish it away or subtly <u>criticize</u> it. I don't need your approval to live my life but I don't appreciate your barrage of snide comments. You are the opposite of a Christian when you do this. You have become small and bitter. I respect you less and less every day.

I <u>did not</u> ruin your life. Your life is your life. I was a part of it for many years, but you made choices on how to become an adult, as did I. You are not a victim of your circumstances. I felt that I was a victim for many years and somehow I turned it around. You have the power to be happy, to create your future. Stop blaming others, you're just lying to yourself.

I have a confession — it's not nice. If I were straight I would have left you years ago, maybe after our son started getting better. The point is that my fear is what kept me in the marriage. We were broken and unhealthy for years and my fear of coming out is what kept me married to you. Because you were a nightmare — your runaway spending was killing me, driving us to bankruptcy. You may have cared for me at one time, but you didn't love me for years. You controlled me. We were a cult and you were the leader. In the end your controlling ways is what finally set me free, brought me to true happiness. I would have stayed married longer, maybe until the kids graduated from high school, but our shitty life is what helped me take a chance. Think about it, you were such a bitch that a closeted fag came out rather than be with you. Face it honey, you fucked up.

I do wish you well despite this rant and my toxic feelings toward you. I want you to have peace, for yourself and for the children. I don't agree with you on many things, but I hope you make better choices. You need to – money, health and happiness are all important and you are on the wrong path on all of them.

You don't care, but I am truly happy now. I am the man I was meant to be. It's not just about being gay. The financial freedom that comes from living within your means is pure bliss. All of my stomach problems are gone! I don't live month-to-month, I save money. Sometimes I even buy myself little things to make me happy. You should try it. And don't talk to me about your budgetary problems – you start each month with over $5,000 in net income and somehow you can't manage. You should be embarrassed and ashamed. Those two emotions consumed me for years and I tried to juggle our money problems. We weren't living, we were surviving. We were faking it – we were on a path to destruction.

You won't believe this, but one of the reasons that I came out was our son. I needed him to see me as a happy gay man and not a couple that is staying together for their children.

Our divorce was another crazy example that I love to share and laugh with my friends. The way that you tried to control that, to demand such crazy shit, is laughable. Who the fuck do you think you are – some type of queen? It's awesome the way that it blew up in your face. And when you sued me three months later, what a fucking joke! You deserved the nothing that you received. Karma's a bitch.

You don't know me anymore, just like I don't know you. I don't need you in my life and frankly, I don't want the current version of you. Maybe we can get to a place where we support each other's lives. I'm ready and willing to do that if things change, but as of now, that won't happen. It'll never happen.

APPENDIX B – *MY FATHER'S LETTER THAT WAS NEVER SENT*

Similar to the ex-wife letter, this was never sent, it was written thirteen years after his death. The previous letter was all about anger for what happened whereas this centers around sadness for what could have been.

I've always wanted to have a heart to heart with you, there are so many questions, so many frustrations that I want to address. I want answers. Let's start with the beginning – who are you? My siblings seem to know the real you and I've been left with nothing, just some vague memories. I feel like I'm the black sheep of the family. I know that your wife favored me over my brother but the reverse was also true. By the way, there was no "winner." My brother is just as fucked up with a lack of approval from his mother as much as I have daddy issues. When I think of my early years and even before the triplets were born, I wonder if you were happy. The house was pretty devoid of love and unfortunately, some of your children's relationships are also crappy. I'm not blaming you for my lot in life – all of us made our own decisions and have the power to make ourselves happy.

Growing up, you were either working or relaxing. I know that working two jobs is incredibly taxing – I can't imagine your commitment to provide for your family, compounded by the lack of love and respect from your wife. You must have been despondent. Ironically, my sister has created the same situation with her husband – they are miserable together. They don't respect each other and are creating a horrible dynamic for their children. And my brother and I married women like our mother – they rule the roost. Funny how history repeats itself.

My high school years was when everything changed. I am forever grateful that you provided me an opportunity to better myself, to break away from the triplets. You did that without guilt. Unfortunately, you also did that without love. I don't recall you ever being proud of me, supporting me emotionally. I'm sure you did in some way, maybe the best way you could, but I didn't feel it then. I don't feel it n ow. I spent most of my high school looking for a father figure – I was constantly latching onto my friend's fathers for their approval, for any emotional support. And I went through periods of hating them as I realized that they had the one thing that I did not, that I would never have. I also started to have feelings about the wrestling coach and my hairy math teacher. I wanted to touch them, for them to touch me. It was confusing and obviously I suppressed it, but I wanted them to like me, I wanted their approval.

And then there is the infamous letter, the one where I asked if you loved me. Looking back now I'm really proud of that Peter – he was scared and made himself vulnerable.

He shared his emotions and that question was a layup. It was a cry for help. And yet, you wouldn't answer it. Can't you see how devastating that would've been for a sensitive boy like me? I'm really disappointed and angry at you for your lack of compassion. I still don't know if you did it on purpose or whether you were unable to deal with the emotions, but that absolutely crushed me. Is it even a question why I blocked you in return? You patently rejected me and I was protecting myself, to prevent you from ever hurting me again. What good did it do me? I don't have a father, no type of legacy to give to my son, my children. I don't know what your goals were as a parent, but I will always feel that you saw the triplets as a mistake, that your life has sucked ever since and that my sister and I are your rejects.

I vowed I would be a different parent. I would be involved where you were not, I would be emotional where you could not. I do regret that I never came out to you, that you never got to see the real me. You saw the dad part of me, which was real and is the true me, but you never got to see the whole me. Me being comfortable with myself. I hate that I don't have anyone to talk about stuff that I like – movies, music, sports and politics. When my siblings talk about their many conversations with you, I feel cheated. What the fuck was so wrong with me? Did you know what you were doing was wrong? Why couldn't you change?

Despite this rambling letter, I don't have any regrets. I did what I thought was best, based on the cards that I was dealt. I do feel bad for you. You missed out on a great guy, a good father. I turned out to be sweet and funny and you never got to know me. As long as they let me, I will be in my children's lives. They will know my friends, they will see me happy, they will see me truly love somebody. In some ways I'm trying to do everything different or the opposite of what you did.

ABOUT THE AUTHOR

A self-proclaimed "ideas guy," I've worked in marketing for over twenty-five years. After years of sadness, emptiness and self-loathing, I finally came out of the closet in 2013 and reinvented myself. Now happily married to my husband for over two years, we live in California with our Chihuahua Felicia, the queen of our household.

Glowing Up Gay is my first book and I hope my journey helps you muster the courage to become the best version of yourself, which may require leaving everything and starting over. Whatever your struggles, there's no reason to handing them along. I hope my story can entice your unique self to break free. Authentic happiness is out there!

https://www.linkedin.com/in/peter-leahy-author

@glowingupgay

glowingupgay@gmail.com

Made in the USA
Columbia, SC
17 June 2025